Critical Media Studies

Volume III

Student Essays on Contemporary Sitcoms

Cover Key

1. Suzanne Warren, *Orange is the New Black*
2. Rebecca Bunch, *Crazy Ex-Girlfriend*
3. Jackie Peyton, *Nurse Jackie*
4. Kimmy Schmidt, *Unbreakable Kimmy Schmidt*
5. Jill Weber, *Odd Mom Out*
6. Grace Hanson, *Grace and Frankie*
7. Daria Morgendorffer, *Daria*
8. Dev Shah, *Master of None*
9. BoJack Horseman, *BoJack Horseman*
10. Louis C.K., *Louie*
11. Frank Gallagher, *Shameless*
12. Tobias Funke, *Arrested Development*
13. Selina Meyer, *Veep*
14. Hannah Horvath, *Girls*

Critical Media Studies

Volume III

Student Essays on Contemporary Sitcoms

by
Wake Forest University Students

edited by
Mary M. Dalton

library partners press
a digital publishing imprint

First Edition

ISBN 978-1-61846-030-1

Copyright © 2017 by the Authors

Cover designed by Kevin Pabst

This work was compiled and edited by Dr. Mary
M. Dalton, Professor of Communication at Wake
Forest University.

Produced and Distributed By:

Library Partners Press
ZSR Library
Wake Forest University
1834 Wake Forest Road
Winston-Salem, North Carolina 27106

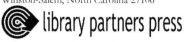

a digital publishing imprint

www.librarypartnerspress.org

Manufactured in the United States of America

ACKNOWLEDGEMENTS

We want to acknowledge those who have helped us produce this anthology. First and foremost, we are grateful to Bill Kane and Library Partners Press for guidance on all matters related to the publication of the book. Without Bill, this project would not have happened.

The faculty and staff at Z. Smith Reynolds Library are beyond compare. Molly Keener advised us ably on copyright and fair use. Our technical consultant Hu Womack led the effort to help us bring images to the book.

The editorial assistance of Caitlin Herlihy helped in the final push to get the volume together; the extra assistance of Max Dosser was greatly appreciated. Max is a veteran of the *Critical Media Studies* series and a co-editor of our second volume in the series, *Student Essays on Deadwood*. Furthermore, our delightful cover design represents the talent of contributor Kevin Pabst.

We appreciate the collegiality of everyone in the Wake Forest University Department of Communication and in the Film and Media Studies Program. Notably, our departmental support staff performs in vital but often invisible ways to support us weekly if not daily. No one keeps us all on track better than Candice Burris and Holly Stearne.

CONTENTS

INTRODUCTION

In April of 1998, I was in a van with three professors from a neighboring university heading to Atlanta, Georgia from our home state of North Carolina to make a presentation at an academic conference. Laura R. Linder and I were in the middle set of seats, and we passed the time pleasantly talking about our respective research projects and creative work. When Laura started telling me about a seminar she had developed on situation comedy (an interest dating to her masters thesis on family sitcoms) and how frustrating it was not to have a good reader to use as a unifying text for the class, I thought of the phrase all young academics hope to encounter – a gap in the literature. I'm not sure where we were when the epiphany struck. Southern North Carolina? South Carolina? I think it probably happened after we crossed the state line somewhere near the iconic water tower in Gaffney, South Carolina that is shaped and painted like a giant peach. At least, that's the way it is written in my mind because of the comic possibilities (I suppose after its cameo in *House of Cards*, we can cite dramatic possibilities, too.) At any rate, we decided that we should produce that book!

By the time Laura and I reached the Georgia state line, we had fleshed out an idea for a critical reader examining the situation comedy, "one of the oldest and most ubiquitous forms of television programming," and we even had settled on a title, *The Sitcom Reader: America Viewed and Skewed*. I don't know how many times we have each taught the sitcom seminar over the years at our respective institutions (I call my iteration of the course Culture and the Sitcom), but many students have used the edited volume as a text, many colleagues have used the book or chapters from it as assigned readings, and Laura and I are especially proud of the second edition of our anthology called *The Sitcom Reader: America*

Re-viewed, Still Skewed. The new edition adopts a chronological approach to organizing our contributors' explorations of identity – race and ethnicity, gender, social class, sexuality, able-bodiedness – historical context, and production practices, examinations they conduct using various critical and theoretical frames.

A couple of years ago, in conjunction with the production of the second edition of *The Sitcom Reader*, I decided to work with Brenda Knox, Director of Online Education at Wake Forest, to create an online version of Culture and the Sitcom and to produce recorded interviews with my co-editor of the volume, Laura, and with our contributing authors. Those interviews have been packaged into a companion website* for *The Sitcom Reader* (https://build.zsr.wfu.edu/sitcomreader) that is available for instructors to use as supplementary viewing for their students, for scholars to use in video or transcript form, and for the public to enjoy for general use. It is my hope that this volume of student essays on contemporary sitcoms will enjoy utility of similar scope and influence. The students whose work is represented in this anthology were part of a special Culture and the Sitcom seminar offered at the graduate level. Their assignment was to engage with the class material – the readings in the anthology, interviews with the contributors to the volume, and assigned episodes to screen – then to use our class discussions as a springboard for their own scholarly inquiry into contemporary sitcoms offered on non-traditional platforms, premium channels, or non-broadcast networks.

In three sections – Form and Function, Bodies of Resistance, From Inside Out – their interests and insights offer a valuable contribution to the literature on the situation comedy. Not surprisingly, the perspective they bring to the (evolving) genre is skeptical about hard and fast rules. They are of the "post" and "trans" generation that sees past boundaries as categorical and entrenched and, instead, views them as constructed and, perhaps even in the best of circumstances, of limited utility. It does not surprise me that many of their essays raise questions about lines drawn in the proverbial sand – lines intended to demarcate conventions of the genre, platforms for distribution, appropriate language, racial identity, old age, gender identity, mental health, and more – and look for meaning(s) and purpose on either side of the (constructed) line.

I find this collection of essays inspiring and useful. It is my intention to include *Student Essays on Contemporary Sitcoms* as a supplemental text for upcoming sections every time I teach Culture and the Sitcom. What better way could there be to help students understand the value of their own research and writing than by taking seriously the scholarship of other students? What better way could there be for me to take seriously my commitment to reciprocal learning than by giving you the opportunity to encounter and interrogate the fresh perspectives of the students featured in this volume? Just as the situation comedy reinvents itself to remain a meaningful part of the media landscape, so must we as fans and readers pay attention to the useful insights of young scholars making their own contributions to the literature on the ubiquitous sitcom. After all, it is our stories that transmit our culture, tell us what it means to be human, and show us our place in the world. Within these popular stories, many an important truth – and sometimes a hidden truth – is revealed in laughter.

*Kyle Denlinger and Benjamin Ellentuck have been instrumental in constructing the companion website.

DEVELOPMENT *UN*-ARRESTED:
CANCELLED SITCOMS MEET STREAMING SERVICES

Max Dosser

1.1 Jason Bateman as Michael Bluth in Arrested Development, "Flight of the Phoenix"

There was an outcry from an admittedly small group of viewers on February 10, 2006, when the series finale of the Emmy-award-winning comedy series *Arrested Development* aired. The sitcom had been cancelled by FOX during its third season. This came as no shock because the series, while critically loved, had low ratings. Still, its audience wanted more, and so did the creative team behind *Arrested Development* (2003-). Their discontent emerges through the dialogue in the show when George Bluth Sr. (Jeffrey Tambor) and Michael Bluth (Jason Bateman) discuss who will buy their failing company. Michael tells him they have not been "bought by HBO" (the Home Buyers Organization), so his father responds, "I guess it's Showtime." This is a thinly veiled comment on how HBO passed on the show, but Showtime seemed like a viable option. Despite the potential interest, creator Mitch Hurwitz decided not to move the show to another network and end the series with the third season (Goodman). The series finale features another meta interaction when Ron Howard (the narrator of the series but in this instance playing himself, a studio executive) tells Maeby Fünke (Alia Shawkat) that her idea for a television series based on her family will not work. He *is* interested in a movie version, however. Despite years of teases about a film, none has been made.

Over seven years after the finale aired, on May 26, 2013, the streaming service Netflix released 15, brand-new episodes of *Arrested Development*. The new fourth season featured the same actors playing the same characters and continued where the third season left off. The revival was commercially successful for Netflix, despite the mixed reception it received from critics and viewers, and led to Netflix reviving other cancelled series such as *Longmire* (2012-) and *Trailer Park Boys* (2001-2016). Other streaming services followed Netflix's lead, and now it is common for showrunners and other producers to shop their cancelled series to streaming services. The practice of reviving series led to a shift in the television environment and fueled the ongoing nostalgia movement seen in the industry. When series are revived on different platforms, they often become entirely different beasts, and the shift can be traced back to how the revival of *Arrested Development* was handled by Netflix.

Arrested Development: Where It All Begins

The first series to be brought back to life in this way (unlike completely altered revivals such as *The New Perry Mason*, which featured a different cast) was the sitcom *Arrested Development*, and through its continuation, we can see the roadmap for how future revivals are handled. As stated earlier, the series never gained much popularity with a broad audience. Instead, it became a cult hit with a small group of rabid fans. One reason why may be that the series was not as accessible as other sitcoms of the time. *Arrested Development* follows the Bluth family after George Bluth Sr., the patriarch of the family and CEO of the Bluth Company, is arrested by the SEC. His arrest means a large portion of the Bluth's assets are frozen. The Bluths are a wealthy, White family that has been rich for so long that the loss of George, Sr. – and more importantly their family fortune – is crippling. The oldest son is G.O.B. (Will Arnett), and he is an amateur magician with no real skills. On the day of the arrest, he accidentally reveals the secret to a trick and is blackballed from the Magician's Alliance, preventing him from performing in the future. In order to upset her parents, the daughter Lindsay (Portia de Rossi) has married Tobias Fünke (David Cross), a man who was once a self-proclaimed analrapist (analyst and therapist). She joins whatever cause most seems to defy her family's wishes. The youngest son, Buster (Tony Hale), has such dramatic mother issues that he has never moved out of the house and depends on his mother for everything from buying his juice to getting from one place to another. He is in his thirties. The mother Lucille (Jessica Walter) is a high functioning alcoholic who seems to hate at least half of her children and wants to continue her lavish lifestyle. Michael, the middle son, is the protagonist and straight man. He wants to run the Bluth Company right and to make sure his own son George Michael (Michael Cera) grows up in a more stable environment than he did. Oh, and George Michal happens to be in love with his cousin, Maeby (Alia Shawkat), who lies her way into a film studio executive job after almost failing her high school classes. As the narrator says in in the opening credits, Michael has no choice but to keep his outlandish and highly dysfunctional family together.

The character descriptions I just provided do not make the Bluths sound like a loveable family. In fact, they seem dysfunctional to the point where viewers might want to look away.

By focusing on the characters perceived to be in the top one percent income bracket of America, specifically a family that constantly uses its wealth to get out of their responsibilities, the series may also have alienated viewers. That feeling of repulsion could be why the series had such low viewership. The viewers who remained, however, were exposed to a hilarious story about a family sticking together. Think *The Royal Tenenbaums* stretched out over 58 episodes minus the fake cancer diagnosis but with the addition of four (and counting) variations of the chicken dance. *Arrested Development* follows Michael and the other Bluths as they try to keep the company afloat, prove the innocence (or guilt in some episodes) of George, Sr., all while developing personal storylines of these seemingly despicable, yet somehow lovable, characters. The series is "a comedy made up of a staggering number of characters, plot points and tones that had no business working together, and yet did. It was a recipe where every ingredient was balanced in perfect proportion to one another" (Sepinwall).

The fourth season of *Arrested Development* received a mixed reception from audience and critics because the show felt changed even though the series featured the same characters in the same world. It felt changed because it *was* changed. The recipe was off. The switch from network to streaming influenced how the series was made. Unlike the previous Netflix series (*House of Cards* (2013-) and *Orange is the New Black*), there was not a bidding war for *Arrested Development*'s fourth season. It was developed specifically for Netflix, which meant the series could take advantage of Netflix's distribution model: the Binge Model. Knowing the entirety of the fourth season would be available instantly meant that if an episode focused entirely on a single character, it was less likely to prevent fans from watching further. Alan Sepinwall pointed this fact out in the second season premiere of *Orange is the*

New Black (2013-). The first season establishes Piper Chapman (Taylor Schilling) in the prison Litchfield. It introduces the audience to that specific prison, including the guards and, more importantly, the ensemble of other prisoners, who are much more lovable than the WASPy Piper. The second season premiere has Piper board a plane and fly to a new prison where she is given new roommates, and the audience is introduced to an entirely new ensemble cast. The characters viewers are accustomed to and love are not featured; instead, the most divisive character is once again the only gateway into this world. Sepinwall points out that because the next episode is only a click away, viewers are able to get back to the characters they care about after a premiere that focuses solely on advancing Piper's storyline (a strategy that may have been influenced by the fourth season of *Arrested Development*) (Sepinwall).

For *Arrested Development*, the change from weekly episodes to the Binge Model meant the entire season could become a single story in which each episode takes place simultaneously with the other episodes. Each episode focuses on a single character rather than the full, ensemble cast, as the series had in the previous three seasons. The only character to appear in every episode is Michael, as his plot involves every family member, while the others are primarily kept to one to three others. Pragmatically, the structure can be explained by the availability of the cast because almost the entire cast became hot commodities after the end of the series. Even so, the fourth season's structure fully utilizes Netflix's model. If an episode featuring only Maeby (one of the less popular characters on the series) had aired on FOX, it is likely even fewer viewers than usual would tune back in the following week. On Netflix, the next episode is a click away, meaning creator Mitch Hurwitz was able to try something new, knowing the audience would keep watching even if he warned viewers not to watch all at once for fear of fatigue (Sepinwall).

The pragmatics and new structure fundamentally change the series including the construction of jokes, development of character arcs, and the reason to re-watch, which left many disappointed (though not this author). In the initial run of the series, running jokes would slip into episodes throughout the course of the season, appearing maybe once every three or four episodes. With the new model, the running jokes would appear three or more times within a single episode because the same character was required for the joke to land. A prime example of this change can be seen with the running jokes involving G.O.B. During the initial run of *Arrested Development*, a running joke (and the one that seems to have made the greatest impact on pop culture) is his phrase "I've made a huge mistake." He says the line in romantic situations – such as when he breaks up with Marta *and* when he gets back together with her – as well as professional ones – such as when he realizes being the CEO of the Bluth Company is more work than he expected. Once the joke is established, other characters start to say it as well. In "Forget-Me-Now" during the third season, G.O.B.'s illegitimate son (and Maeby's crush) Steve Holt (Justin Grant Wade) comes to G.O.B. for advice, believing he has slept with his cousin. Steve says he has "made a huge mistake." G.O.B., with an unexpected father-like compassion (at first), tells him, "I know the feeling. I had you." It should also be said that in addition to G.O.B. being a mediocre (at best) magician, he is also a terrible and inattentive father. The joke takes on a life of its own over the first three seasons during which the line appears 15 different times.

In contrast, the fourth season introduces a running joke with the Simon & Garfunkel song "Sound of Silence." When G.O.B. has a moment of realization (often about something in his romantic life advancing past a point where he would like it to), the camera slowly zooms in on his sullen face as Simon and Garfunkel begin to sing "Hello, darkness, my old friend. I've come to talk with you again." It is a brief interlude showing viewers the emotional toll of G.O.B.'s decisions on him, but once he snaps out of his reverie, he is back to his normal, obnoxiously ignorant, self-indulgent persona. The joke lands well every time, and like the "I've made a huge mistake" joke, it begins to happen with other characters, like rival magician Tony Wonder (Ben Stiller). A primary difference is that rather than spreading the joke out fifteen times over 58 episodes, this joke happens five times in the two G.O.B.-centric episodes. The compression is necessary as G.O.B. is only prominently featured in two episodes, but it is also indicative of the Binge Model in which episodes are watched in a few sittings rather than multiple months so that the frequency of running jokes and character beats featuring them need to decrease in order not to become tedious for the audience.

The compression of the running jokes also means that plots develop in different ways. Some are more expedient, and some are slower. Season-long arcs are present in both the initial run of *Arrested Development* and the Netflix season. In the first season, Michael works to gather evidence to prove his father is innocent. The climax of the season is Michael, having decided his father is guilty, refusing to take a polygraph test. Instead, George, Sr. takes it, fakes a heart attack, and then escapes from the hospital. He winds up hiding in the attic where the majority of the Bluths are staying, and Michael finds him there. Given the chance to turn him in, Michael decides to keep his father hidden, thinking there actually is a chance he may be innocent. It is the emotional payoff of a season built around the tension between father and son as well as the disruption of a season featuring George, Sr. in prison. Similarly, the Netflix season features Michael trying to get the signatures of his family members so Ron Howard (again, playing himself) can make a movie based on the Bluth family. In the first episode, Michael tells his family he is done with them and moves away, attempting to cut ties. Events during the season force Michael to make amends (then break them again as he rips up each character's signature) with the family he thought was comprised of nothing but screw ups only to climax with him owing a dangerous family $70,000, which demonstrates that the apple falls closer to the tree than he claimed originally.

Both seasons feature emotional and plot payoffs involving Michael, but the seasons diverge when it comes to the other Bluths. An example is Buster, who only receives a single episode during the fourth season. In the second season, Buster has a variety of plot lines going: his romance with Lucille Austero (Liza Minnelli), being enlisted in the army, struggling over his relationship with his mother, and finding out the identity of his true father. Stretched out over eighteen episodes, there are some episodes featuring Buster struggling to decide whether he is actually interested in Lucille Austero (usually called Lucille Two) romantically or if she just reminds him of his mother, others in which he is training for the army or trying to get out of his assignment (only to have his hand bitten off by a loose seal in a yellow bowtie), and still others during which he rebels against his mother only to try to win her back by the end of the half hour. The season culminates with Buster finding out Oscar Bluth, his father's twin (also played by Jeffrey Tambor), is his biological father. When he confronts his mother, she cannot explain why she hid the truth, so Buster moves out. It is an emotional climax to two of his main storylines with the army and romance plots carrying over to the third (and fourth) seasons.

Buster's plot in the fourth season is dramatically compressed; he is only featured in a single, spotlight episode. Still, this episode touches on three of the four plotlines from the second season, as Buster gets in a fight with his mother only to be lured over to Lucille Two's apartment. She gets him drunk on juice, and he misses his mother's trial, which causes a new rift between the two. His mother does not allow him to visit her even after he is forced to rejoin the army where he crashes while flying a virtual drone (he falls out of his chair). The army blows the incident out of proportion, takes him to the hospital, and gives him a new hand. The hand is robotic and giant – so large, in fact, that he feels even more freakish than he did with the hook. He is welcomed in by Herbert Love's (Terry Crews) family. Love is a right-wing politician running for Congress against Lucille Two, and he thinks having an injured veteran on the campaign with him will be a boost. Buster ends up sleeping with Love's wife, who craves emotional attention since her husband is always gone. Buster, as is his way, has been treating her like a mother. His episode climaxes with his ejection from the Love household, his assault of Herbert Love, and his arrest as a suspect in Lucille Two's disappearance. Did I mention all of that happens in 36 minutes? Buster's episode, like those featuring the other characters, continue storylines and themes from the initial run of the series, but the plots are compressed into one or two episodes rather than being able to play out over a season.

With the simultaneous release of the entire season, the series is also able to obfuscate and misdirect the audience in new ways. The fourth season feels like a puzzle for which viewers need all the pieces to fully understand the plot and even to get some of the jokes. During the first season, when G.O.B.'s girlfriend mentions being in love with "Hermano," the audience immediately makes the connection that the *hermano* (Spanish for brother) is Michael, which allows dramatic irony to fuel the Marta arc of the first season. In first episode of the Netflix season, George Michael mentions he has software called Fakeblock. It is hinted throughout the season that Fakeblock is a privacy software, but it is not revealed until near the finale what the software actually is.

This makes the fourth season a puzzle that can be appreciated differently upon repeat viewings. Repeat viewings of the initial run of *Arrested Development* create a similar feeling, but it is primarily because many seemingly throwaway jokes actually foreshadow upcoming events. When Buster wins a stuffed seal out of a claw machine, for example, and the narrator says, "Buster had gotten hooked playing," this foreshadows Buster's hand being bitten off by the seal then replaced by a hook in the season finale. During the Netflix season, foreshadowing as a narrative device is inverted; rather than hinting at what will come, each episode of the series reveals why characters are not present for an important event in the series.

In the first episode, Lucille is put on trial for stealing the Queen Mary and requests that her family come to the trial to testify she only stole the ship to save her poor son Buster, who had fallen overboard (which is, of course, a lie). The actual trial is not shown until Lucille's individual episode, the tenth of the season, but the audience is shown episode by episode why each family member misses the trial from G.O.B. being trapped in a storage locker to Lindsay working on an ostrich farm to Buster being "hung over" from drinking too much sugar-free juice (which was not actually sugar free). It is clear that no one appears to testify from the beginning of the season, but rather than foreshadow the trial, the episodes fill in the gaps for why no one appears. In a Binge Model, the obscure jokes are more apparent, and the climax comes as less of a surprise. The change to making the season a puzzle allows Mitch Hurwitz to create a new reason for these episodes to be viewed more than once so viewers can see how the pieces fit together once they know how it all ends. None of the structural changes are necessarily positive or negative. Rather, the changes illustrate how a series morphs as it transitions from being a network sitcom to fit the Binge Model when revived by a streaming service.

Those Who Follow

While it is not necessarily unprecedented, or even uncommon, for networks and cable to revive cancelled series, Netflix doing so with *Arrested Development* lit a match in the industry that caused other streaming services to fly into the flame. Series like *Futurama* (1999-2013) and *Cougar Town* (2009-15) were cancelled by FOX and ABC only to be brought back to life on Comedy Central and TBS, respectively. Even though Showtime showed interest in *Arrested Development*, it was less likely to happen for cult series than for those with wider viewership because networks and cable have "to thread the needle of being able to fit [their] brands" (Wallenstein 34). Networks and cable are forced to produce what appeals to their specific audiences, which is why CBS continues to make multi-cam sitcoms like *The Big Bang Theory* (2007-) and *Mom* (2013-) and why FOX continues producing raunchy, animated series focused on families like the Griffins (*Family Guy*) and the Simpsons (*The Simpsons*). Streaming services have an eclectic catalog because their viewers come from all walks of life. Due to this, streaming services cannot develop a specific brand and are able to practice narrowcasting to appeal to every niche within their wider audiences. The depth of their catalogs means they need diversity in their offerings. This need is why Netflix is able to create children's series based off DreamWorks Animation product like *Dragons: Race to the Edge* (2015-) and *Trollhunters* (2016-) alongside the political drama *House of Cards* (2013-), the superhero series *Marvel's Daredevil* (2015-) and *Marvel's Jessica Jones* (2015-), revived series *Arrested Development*, and more.

After the success of *Arrested Development*, other streaming services like Hulu and Yahoo! Video followed Netflix's lead and began reviving cancelled series. Oftentimes, series were saved from the brink of cancellation, like *The Mindy Project* (2012-) with Hulu or *Community* (2009-2015) with Yahoo! Video; each had gained a small, yet passionate, following before being cancelled due to low ratings. Other times, the stories are more similar to *Arrested Development*'s in which the revived series had been cancelled years prior. An example from Netflix is *Gilmore Girls: A Year in the Life* (*Gilmore Girls* nine years later). These revivals are fueled by nostalgia because the original series were cancelled after many years on the air with strong fan bases intact; in some cases, the popularity of the shows has grown since the series ended due to repeats of episodes on the air and streaming availability.

Similar to the fourth season of *Arrested Development*, these revived/continued series changed as they transitioned from network television to streaming service properties. The changes either correspond directly to those of the fourth season of *Arrested Development* or are structured to try to avoid the criticisms of the fourth season. Some of the alterations are smaller, like not breaking for commercials and expanding lengths, which is part of the Netflix model. *Community* and *The Mindy Project* were revived by streaming services that decided to keep the weekly release model. In this way, both series avoid the problem *Arrested Development* encountered where running jokes would need to be reduced because as the audience would grow tired of them. *Community* encountered a similar issue of cast availability. One of the main criticisms lobbed at the fourth season of *Arrested Development* was how the spotlight episodes eliminate the interactions among the characters, which has always been a highlight of the series (Poniewozik). *Community*, a sitcom about an unlikely group of friends attending the fictional community college Greendale, had received similar praise for its cast, but by the time Hulu aired the first episode of season six, the central study group has dropped from seven to four. In addition to losing main characters, prominent tertiary characters have also disappeared and leave Greendale feeling like a ghost town. Seeing how *Arrested Development* handles its character flexibility, *Community* brings in new characters to fill out the cast. Introducing new characters makes the series feel further removed from its original form, but it allows a core cast to appear in every episode rather than having some characters pop in and out based on the actors' availability. The Yahoo! TV *Community* season handles the arcs of the characters differently, similar to *Arrested Development*, as the season is structured to bring the series to a close, which means character development needs to be compressed to resolve the storylines of various characters by the end of a season.

    The Mindy Project changed in many ways as well, like shifting to a more natural three act-structure after suffering under the enforced four-act structure while airing on FOX. Streaming on Hulu meant it was underwent many of the same changes as *Community*, which had a similar distribution model as Yahoo! TV. Both series kept central plot elements from their initial runs, so even as the structure, format, release schedule, and cast change, the series feels largely the same as before. This is the same as *Arrested Development* in which each episode is the natural (usually) progression of the character's story from the end of the initial run. While the Yahoo! TV season of *Community* and the Hulu seasons of *The Mindy Project* aired a year after their cancellations rather than several years afterward, the blueprint of *Arrested Development*'s Netflix season is clearly visible in the construction of these series.

    While *Community* and *The Mindy Project* are examples of cancelled series brought back shortly after cancellation, *Arrested Development*'s impact may be more apparent in long ago cancelled series, like *Gilmore Girls: A Year in the Life*, which is set nine years after the end of *Gilmore Girls*. The dramedy about a 30-something single mother and her teenage daughter was cancelled a season after a contract dispute led to the creator leaving, so the story was left unfinished. Much like *Arrested Development*, the series picks up where it left off with little development happening for the characters between the point where the series ended and where the revival begins. The main difference is that *Gilmore Girls* is comprised of seven, 22-episode seasons while *Gilmore Girls: A Year in the Life* is only one season made up of four, 90-minute episodes. The compression to four longer episodes was largely due to cast availability, and being a Netflix series, the producers were likely concerned with similar criticisms as *Arrested Development*. This meant the *Gilmore Girls* revival faced the same issues of plot compression and running gags as *Arrested Development*.

The daughter, Rory Gilmore (Alexis Bledel), starts out as a journalist published in *The New Yorker* to becoming the editor of her hometown's newspaper (Stars Hollow) as well as repeating her mother's mistakes by falling for an unavailable man. Her mother, Lorelai Gilmore (Lauren Graham), marries her long-term boyfriend and finally achieves a form of reconciliation with her mother after a lifetime of issues. All these plotlines would be season-long (if not series-long) plotlines, but they are compressed into the four episodes. It makes certain points (like Rory's career) feel rushed while others (like Lorelai's reconciliation) feel like the series is coming to a close. New running jokes (like Lorelai wanting to replicate the journey in *Wild*) are made in the first episode and paid off by the fourth, rather than being stretched out over the 22-episodes. The season builds to the series finale, so throughout the four episodes, there are hints of foreshadowing for the final four words creator Amy Sherman-Palladino thought of early in the series (no spoilers), whereas earlier seasons do not employ foreshadowing and attempt to live more in the moment. Each change from the original series to the revival correlates with a change made in the Netflix season of *Arrested Development*.

The changes in all of the series mentioned above can be seen as pragmatic because streaming services have different practices and standards than networks, but at a certain point, when everything is changing based on practicality, one cannot dismiss the importance of the pragmatics. Through tracking these series and their revivals and seeing how the narrative trajectories parallel those of *Arrested Development*, it is clear this Netflix revival has had a strong influence on the television industry. *Arrested Development* will continue to have a significant impact as more and more revivals and continuations are greenlit.

Fueled By Nostalgia

The television environment continues to change, so the question becomes what are the implications related to format moving forward? Netflix began changing the environment with *Arrested Development*, but it went a step further with another series. *Unbreakable Kimmy Schmidt* is about a woman who is released from an underground bunker after a reverend has held her captive there for 15 years under the delusion that the world has ended. The show was originally developed for NBC because the creators, Tina Fey and Robert Carlock, had a strong relationship with that network built upon the success of *30 Rock*, another insanely hilarious but low-rated sitcom. When network executives realized *Unbreakable Kimmy Schmidt* would not fit into their programming lineup (the Thursday night comedy block had just been removed from the schedule), Netflix bought the series. NBC would have almost certainly cancelled the show. It was a niche series that would likely have gathered critical adoration and gain a cult following but – like *Arrested Development*, *Community*, and *The Mindy Project* – would never have attracted a wide audience. Due to its high potential for cancellation, one could argue (and I do) that a streaming service saved a series yet again. *Unbreakable Kimmy Schmidt* has thrived on Netflix, gathering a sizable audience and accolades from critics, the public, and the Television Academy. The preemptive salvation of series may become commonplace for streaming services as they continue to grow their libraries to fill the needs of niche audiences, but the effects have rippled beyond the streaming services. The results have become evident among broadcast and cable stations as well.

As with *Arrested Development*, which Brian Lowry of *Variety* claims was created so the audience could "bask in the nostalgia," a wave of nostalgia has begun to fuel television production (Lowry). Networks, cable, and streaming services alike are rebooting cancelled series and films so they will have established intellectual property with existing fan bases on the air/internet. These reboots can exist as limited series – like *Gilmore Girls: A Day in the Life* – or they can be the start of a long running series – like Netflix's *Fuller House* (a revival/continuation of the sitcom *Full House* that focuses on the grown-up daughters). Examples of limited series include: *Heroes: Reborn* (from the cancelled *Heroes*), *24: Live Another Day* (from the cancelled *24*), and *The X-Files* (from the cancelled series of the same title). Similar to *Fuller House*, Amazon picked up the 2001 sitcom *The Tick* (which had previously run three seasons as an animated series) with an order for a full season slated to appear in 2017. As of this writing, CBS has *MacGyver* back on the air. Even *24*, which received *24: Live Another Day* as a limited series continuation, is being rebooted as *24: Legacy* now that the star is done with the series. The revivals are not restricted to cancelled television series; FOX airs a series based on the *Lethal Weapon* film franchise. These series tap into narratives America wants to see: the same things viewers already knew they liked. The fact that

Arrested Development's fourth season was so popular and commercially successful, even though it received a mixed reception, reassured networks, cable, and streaming services that there is a market on television for revivals and reboots.

These revivals, reboots, and continuations are becoming more and more prevalent as film and television industry executives realize that the American viewer becomes more deeply entrenched in a love affair with nostalgia each year. The pattern is evident in the success of series that recall previous times (see *Stranger Things* and the 1980s), but it also plays out in how 1990s sitcoms and 2000s dramas are given new life and often resurrected with the same creative teams that helmed the originals. It is a pattern repeated in film as well as television. Year around, multiplexes are filled with sequels (like the new *Star Wars* films), prequels (also the new *Star Wars* films), reboots (*Ghostbusters*), and movies based on intellectual property (almost any superhero film). In the weeks leading up to this volume's release, announcements have come that CBS wants to reboot *The Honeymooners* (a problematic sitcom from 1955 about a blue-collar family), Disney plans to reboot *Ducktales* (an animated series about the misadventures of Donald Duck's nephews and their wealthy uncle Scrooge McDuck), and that Disney plans to produce a *Fuller House*-style continuation of *That's So Raven* (a sitcom about a teenage psychic navigating her social life with the power of premonition) featuring the eponymous Raven (Raven Symoné) as an adult who has a psychic child of her own. When networks are reaching back to the 1950s for some of their reboots, it is clear it is not a passing trend. The origin of a series has no direct impact on quality, whether it is a revival, reboot, or continuation. Some examples are exceptional – *Star Wars* films, many of the revived sitcoms (*Arrested Development*, in this author's opinion), and rebooted series (*Fargo*, a limited series loosely based on the Coen Brothers's film) fall into this category – while other projects hardly seem the effort. Even so, with 412 scripted series on the air last year, the revivals, reboots, and continuations do not seem too overwhelming (Malone 11). At least, not yet.

Conclusion

The environment of television is changing rapidly, and we are able to see a marked transition starting with *Arrested Development*'s fourth season on Netflix. Many of the series being written about in this volume exist due to the expansion of streaming services and the power those platforms have to bring the dead back to life (or to the air/web in this case). Cancellations no longer mean the death of a series, but revivals do not promise the same show will return. The increase in the amount of television produced has led to this ever-growing subset of revivals and reboots, many using the pull of nostalgia to draw in viewers. The impact of these series and their deep-pocketed streaming homes has already been felt, but it has only been three years since *Arrested Development* returned to the small screen. Who knows what the medium we still call television will be by the time the fifth season is released?

1.2 Will Arnett as GOB Bluth in Arrested Development, "Colony Collapse"lockheads"

NEVER LETTING GO:
REDEFINING THE *CRAZY EX-GIRLFRIEND* AND
WHAT IT MEANS TO BE HAPPY

Callie Sartain

2.1 Rachel Bloom as Rebecca Bunch in Crazy Ex-Girlfriend, "Josh Just Happens to Live Here!"

Despite initial low ratings, the CW's musical romantic comedy *Crazy Ex-Girlfriend* (2015-) has managed to flourish. Created by and starring Rachel Bloom, the series centers around a young New York attorney who finds herself questioning the sources of her unhappiness after a happenstance encounter with an ex-boyfriend from a junior high summer camp experience. Despite its apparent irrationality, Rebecca Bunch (Rachel Bloom) finds herself struck by the realization that her life in the big city, while financially gratifying, is less-than-satisfactory, and she impulsively decides to pack up her apartment to follow this ex-boyfriend, Josh Chan (Vincent Rodriguez, III), to the epitome of American humdrum suburbia: West Covina, California. The show finds success in a variety of outlets: the musical numbers are clever and capable of advancing an entertaining plot, the cast comes across as organic and relatable, and Rebecca employs just the right amount of self-deprecation to make her a character worth rooting for, despite her frequent cringe-inducing choices. But the show's true success, the one that merits the most critical acclaim, is the witty-yet-powerful dialogue constructed to explore the ways in which the quest for happiness goes unfulfilled when that exploration is based upon ill-conceived notions of what it means to be happy.

In *Happy Objects,* Sarah Ahmed invites us to understand happiness as a feeling or state of being that "turns us towards objects" (29). By this standard, she writes "to be made happy by this or that is to recognize that happiness starts from somewhere other than the subject who may use the word to describe a situation" (Ahmed 30). This certainly seems to be the case for Rebecca, who turns toward objects (Josh, West Covina) as means by which she hopes to obtain happiness. The show opens with Rebecca turning down an offer to be made junior partner at the prestigious law firm where she works. In pondering the possibilities that will inevitably follow the acceptance of such a position, Rebecca takes a breather outside her office and notices a butter advertisement that begs her consideration of the question, "When was the last time you were truly happy?" In response, she seeks support from two sources: prayers to a divine being she may or may not actually believe in and her anti-anxiety medication. The combination of such a profound question and a subsequent run-in with ex-boyfriend Josh piques Rebecca's interest enough for her to reevaluate her life in a way that necessitates packing up all of her belongings to follow him to West Covina, California – a place in which, he claims, everyone is happy. Plus, as noted in the pilot episode, it's "only two hours from the beach!" Rebecca begins to view this pursuit of her old flame as the solution to the depression and anxiety that has tormented her since childhood. The fact that Josh is in a serious relationship with another woman doesn't deter her, and neither does the glaring reality that the two dated briefly, nearly a decade ago during summer camp, while both were adolescents.

Crazy-Ex Girlfriend joins a fairly small pool of musical comedies on television, the likes of which include more recent programs such as *Garfunkel and Oats, Flight of the Conchords,* and *Galavant.* The format of the show differs fairly significantly from many of the musical shows that preceded it decades before in that the musical numbers serve as embellishments rather than the main attraction of the series. Each episode of *Crazy Ex-Girlfriend* features an average of two to three musical numbers, most of which are written by Rachel Bloom as complements to the emotional high points and low points of each episode. Rebecca Bunch is the main focus of most (but not all) of the musical numbers, and they often serve as commentary on her interactions with other characters. The pilot episode, originally set to premiere on *Showtime,* was picked up by the CW in early 2015 and reworked extensively to both lengthen the show from a half hour to a full hour and also to appeal to a larger audience of broadcast network consumers. The musical nature of the show is fairly unique to the CW, and the initially less-than-stellar ratings can perhaps be attributed to what Richard Hornby describes as an audience's tendency to view musicals as "too obviously pleasurable, too much fun to be taken seriously as drama" (1988). This is unfortunate, Hornby argues, as the musical theatre genre has just as much potential to tackle some of the most significant cultural mores of our time as any other genre. *Crazy Ex-Girlfriend* does just that in ways that are equal parts eloquent, insightful, and charmingly absurd. "The Sexy Getting Ready Song" addresses the patriarchal nature of women's grooming customs (complete with references to Simone de

Beauvoir's *The Second Sex*), "Gettin' Bi" normalizes the coming out process for bisexual individuals ("It's not a phase/ I'm not confused/ Not indecisive/ I don't have the 'gotta choose blues!'"), and "Sexy French Depression" spoofs the trope of glamorized depression.

"West Covina," the opening song of the pilot episode, is perhaps one of the kitschiest and stereotypical musical numbers of the series, but this song introduces viewers to just how irrational Rebecca's decision to move across the country truly is. For Rebecca, West Covina represents an opportunity to escape the hopelessness and despair that has become her life in New York City. The fact that Josh just so happens to live there as well is Rebecca's idea of a coincidental bonus, not the primary impetus of her decision. The song, despite its Disney-esque music and showy dance routines, serves to illuminate the obvious dullness of what Rebecca desperately refers to as "the pride of the inland empire," particularly in contrast to the excitement of a place like New York City. "West Covina" also makes obvious the reality that Rebecca's primary motivation for moving to California *is* Josh Chan, who represents for her a prospective romantic partner on the surface and, more intrinsically, a chance to finally answer the "When was the last time you were truly happy" question prompted repeatedly by the butter advertisement. It also becomes clear in this moment that what drives Rebecca to begin rewriting her story is not just Josh the *person* but Josh the *idea*, an idea that motivates her to believe she can disentangle herself from reality and construct a version of herself she hadn't been able to find on her own.

While the first couple of episodes might imply that the series is, at its core, just about a woman who embodies the "crazy ex-girlfriend" archetype and the shenanigans that follow her, the scope of the show actually extends much further. For Rebecca, Josh represents more than just an ex-boyfriend to be won over; he represents the possibilities that accompany a life uninhibited by the burdens of depression and anxiety. In other words, he represents a kind of happiness that Rebecca would have the potential to experience if she weren't so consumed by false notions of satisfaction. Rebecca is so sure that her relocation (which really means, essentially, running away from her lackluster life in New York instead of confronting her depression head on) will bring her contentment that she flushes her anxiety medicine down the sink upon arrival in California. From this point forward, all of Rebecca's decisions become motivated by the prospect of getting back together with Josh, though she denies it repeatedly and vehemently (from the pilot episode: "To be clear, I didn't move here for Josh, I just needed a change/ 'Cause to move here for Josh, now that'd be strange"). Despite the fact that her protestations read as a desperate attempt to mask her true intention in moving, perhaps there is some truth to this lyric; Rebecca is surely smart enough to recognize the unabashed absurdity of moving across the country for a person she once dated as a teenager, and a change in her life could certainly do her some good. The fact that she is so dedicated to this one particular life script, however, prevents her from making any kind of emotional progress and inhibits her from recognizing the sources from which authentic happiness can come, the likes of which might not necessarily include Josh. Happiness, or at least Rebecca's convoluted definition of it, becomes her goal as opposed to her method.

Rebecca is so fixated on the hope that West Covina will fulfill something she has been missing her whole life that she inadvertently blinds herself to the many ways she is creating a potentially fulfilling new life for herself separate from Josh. Upon arrival in West Covina, she befriends the cute bartender Greg Serrano (Santino Fontana) who, similarly to Rebecca, spends a significant amount of time seeking ways to sooth his troubled soul (though he is undoubtedly much more rational in these endeavors than Rebecca). The two strike up what can only be described as an on-again/off-again "flirtationship" in which they occasionally explore the possibility of being together but ultimately end up on different pages until the very end of the season. Though Greg is certainly irritable and struggles with his own woes, he invests in Rebecca multiple times and shows that he cares for her in ways that Josh does not. Rebecca continues to write him off as a sort of obstacle to overcome in her pursuit of Josh, which causes temporary strife between the two. It isn't until the fourteenth episode ("Why is Josh in a Bad Mood?") that Rebecca realizes she might, in fact, want to reciprocate the feelings that Greg has shown her. "Oh My God I Think I Like You" details the realization that not only is she physically attracted to Greg, but perhaps she feels an emotional connection as well: "But I say no, no, no!/ This is just about sex!/ Don't be such a girl, Bex!/ But then I feel the Oxytocin creeping back to my brain,/ And all I can do it sing it again,/ Oh my God, I think I like you." Rebecca is presented in her most contented state during moments like these when her attention is not entirely consumed by someone who is both emotionally and platonically unavailable. And yet, she is still unsatisfied because the way she defines happiness leads to a relationship with Josh, not with Greg. NPR's Linda Holmes writes a metaphor is apropos for the situation and also feels appropriate for a musical television comedy: "It's as if Rebecca bought a dilapidated house so she could grow pineapples outside. And even though it turned out she couldn't grow pineapples, she fixed up the house beautifully, only to spend all her time staring out the window and being sad about failing." In other words, Rebecca finds someone with whom she is compatible, someone who cares about her and is willing to invest in her, and yet—he isn't Josh. Therefore, in Rebecca's world, this isn't happiness, and she is left unsatisfied yet again.

Rebecca's convoluted belief in love's ability to cure unhappiness becomes increasingly clearer as the series unfolds. In episode 14 of first season, after multiple attempts to win his favor and attention, Rebecca experiences a small victory in her discovery that Josh actually has mixed feelings about her. This may be where Rebecca comes closest to recognizing her delusions about happiness, the havoc these delusions have wreaked upon her live and the lives of others, and some of the consequences of her misguided thinking. Above all, she begins to recognize that her efforts to win Josh's love have been, quite frankly, manipulative and inappropriately desperate. The sinister number "I'm the Villain in My Own Story," which is found in the episode "Josh is Going to Hawaii," channels a stereotypical Disney villain aesthetic and narrates Rebecca's realization that she has rendered herself the antagonist of her own story, a narrative in which she previously perceived herself to be the victim. In the musical number, Rebecca is depicted as an insanely unattractive witch who holds Josh's girlfriend Valencia Perez (Gabrielle Ruiz) hostage, revealing "I'm jealous of you and your life!/ You're so skinny and Josh is so perfect/ And I want to take it all for myself!"

Affect Theory is a helpful theoretical framework for exploring the motivations behind Rebecca's unrelenting efforts to win Josh's love despite her consistent lack of success. The founder of Affect Theory, Silvan Tomkins, introduces the idea of Affect as that which motivates with a sense of urgency unlike anything else within the human condition and considers it to be "the primary innate biological motivating mechanism, more urgent than drive deprivation and pleasure, and more urgent than even physical pain" (Tomkins 163). Under the directions of Affect, little else has the capacity to matter. The theory is particularly relevant to Rebecca's decisions because the theory quite literally emerged from the margins in response to the academic preference for rationality over emotion. In the same way, Rebecca's move to West Covina functions as a decision made in direct contrast to rational decision making. Pragmatically speaking, Rebecca has followed all of society's instructions for achieving happiness, the least of which includes a high-paying career at a prominent law firm and an Ivy League education. And yet, she remains totally and completely unsatisfied with her life, a dilemma that can be potentially elucidated through an affective theoretical lens. Essentially, affect theory stems ontologically from the perspective that feelings matter; they are persuasive, they are real, and they are used in significant ways to affect decision making in substantial ways. Ahmed explores how "happiness functions as a promise that directs us toward certain objects," a view that necessitates thinking of affect as "sticky" and capable of producing a rhetorical residue that sticks to a person long after a decision is made.

Life near Josh in West Covina becomes Rebecca's definition of happiness despite the unreliability of the man or the location to fit her preconceptions, all of which cleverly emphasizes the problematic aspects of relying on romantic relationships as a means of happiness. In a piece on individualism within contemporary romantic relationships, Daniel Santore argues the ways in which romantic relationships have evolved to encourage individual agency, "implying that the negotiation of intimacy has become an increasingly 'do-it-yourself' project" (Santore 1202). Further, he argues, contemporary romantic relationships have developed into one of the few manageable aspects of an individual's life, particularly in the wake of "new uncertainties" such as "work and psychosocial uncertainty" (Santore 1203). In this sense, we can understand Rebecca's quest for happiness (in the form of a relationship with Josh) as her own sort of do-it-yourself project undertaken in the midst of the kind of uncertainty that often accompanies life in a new city, interacting with new friends, and employment in a new workplace environment.

Though Josh occupies the majority of Rebecca's attention and provides much of the plot content, it becomes quite apparent that Rebecca's desire for both a fresh start and a romantic relationship are driven by other factors as well. NPR entertainment critic Linda Holmes writes that the move to West Covina was less about actually being obsessed or in love with Josh than about the idea that "life with him was unbounded by reality – by any reality at all." It is this sort of "adaptive foolishness" that allows Rebecca to continue a relentless pursuit of happiness, and yet she never seems to find it. Holmes suggests that perhaps Rebecca never reaches happiness not because she doesn't end up with Josh but because she is so completely absorbed in happiness as an objective that she fails to see the ways in which her new life in West Covina is capable of providing sources of fulfillment outside of a relationship. In other words, as Holmes writes, "she's winning where she's not looking." Rebecca seems to realize this eventually, however, and at some point during the first season begins to realize that her obsession with Josh as an Affective object is destined for failure. In "That Text Was Not Meant for Josh," which falls near the middle of the season, Rebecca expresses her frustration with herself ("You ruined everything/ You stupid bitch") and sings: "I was so close to paradise/ But now the only thing I'm close to is defeat./ These shards are a metaphor for my soul/ Won't stop the self-pity 'cause I'm on a roll,/ Yes Josh completes me, but how can that be/ When there's no me left to complete?"

Rebecca's somewhat manic concentration on Josh as an objective leads her to pull all kinds of over-the-top stunts in the hopes of winning his attention and affection. Such a heightened sense of focus significantly clouds her judgment and makes it impossible for her to acknowledge that the new life she has created for herself in West Covina actually has more potential to inform her happiness than any kind of relationship with Josh might. She's arguably the most accomplished and talented attorney at her second-tier law firm, she's forged new and meaningful relationships with multiple characters (most prominently co-worker Paula, played by Donna Lynne Champlin), and she seems to be spending more time engaged in meaningful activities than she ever did in New York City. And yet, happiness continues to elude her. Josh is not quite yet a permanent romantic fixture in her life and, as a consequence, Rebecca continues to find herself unable to determine "the last time [she was] truly happy" as prompted by the butter commercial that seems to appear at the most opportune times. Halfway through the season, though, Rebecca appears to give up hope on Josh and, ironically, it is during this time that she appears to be the most content with her life. With Josh on the backburner, Rebecca develops a greater appreciation of the new life and the relationships she has built in West Covina. Whether or not she acknowledges it (or even recognizes it), this is where Rebecca is most likely to find true happiness.

Soon after sound came to the movies (1927) and long before television arrived on the scene, musicals emerged as a favorite form of escapist entertain during the Great Depression. Elaborate musical numbers took center stage in these early films, and people fell in love in formulaic backstage dramas. Musicals became more complex over the years, but most of the conventions of the genre have remained familiar if not predictable. Born in the Great Depression, the genre has been inverted in this series to deal with lowercase depression and other significant issues long marginalized while also creating a hybrid form in the musical-sitcom expanded to fit an hour-long television format. The surprise is not that someone decided to go bold and experiment with content and form this way but that it works so well. The show has style, but it also has substance. Despite a title that seems an affront to the eponymous character and the occasional silliness of an over-the-top musical number, *Crazy Ex-Girlfriend* digs deeply into the myriad of ways in which happiness both evades us and presents itself to us. For Rebecca Bloom, happiness only appears in the form of a fantasized relationship with Josh, an objective that consumes all of her time and energy. Despite her inability to recognize this, it is apparent that opportunities for genuine happiness are all around her; they appear in the form of a meaningful friendship with Paula, success at her law firm, and an ability to address and overcome deep emotional wounds inflicted by her mother (Tovah Feldsuh). Her obliviousness to the ability that rests within herself to lead a happy life is what prevents her from doing so, and the show masterfully explores this dilemma in a way that is both smart and invites easy identification from viewers. If happiness is understood as "a condition that must be prepared for, cultivated and defended privately by each person," it would seem as though Rebecca has quite a long journey ahead of her (Csikszentmihali). Perhaps the show's second season will allow her character to continue evolving in a way that might eventually encourage her to reevaluate her ability to find happiness without necessitating that it appear in the form of Josh. Until then, I'll continue to root for her and to sing along. As noted above, the show has style, but does it have legs? Used in the showbiz tradition to connote longevity, only time will tell whether the series continues to be as successful, engaging, and meaningful as its significant first season.

WHAT THE *VEEP?* :
CURSING, CONTRADICTIONS, AND AMERICAN POLITICIANS

Karoline Summerville

3.1 Julia Louis-Dreyfus as Selina Meyer and Tony Hale as Gary Walsh in Veep,
"Tears"

After the terrorist attacks on September 11, 2001, Americans became overwhelmingly cynical and full of mistrust toward the government and the media. In the midst of a "War on Terror" and an economic crisis, America was in dire need of some comic relief. As a result, satirical news shows like *The Daily Show* and *The Colbert Report*, comedy shows like *Saturday Night Live*, and late night talk shows rose in popularity (Guggenheim, Kwak, and Campbell, 277). Political satire became a subversive outlet for many Americans who no longer believed in a government for the people and by the people. Viewers no longer put their faith in government; instead, they invested in laughter. Being connected required motivated citizens to stay involved for the sake of being in on the joke instead of the punch line because many satirical shows relied on viewers understanding the complex relationships among politicians, the media, and the public. Satirical shows also give politicians a chance to mend the relationship between the government and the public. Many political figures, including Hillary Clinton, Barack Obama, and Donald Trump have partnered with satirical television programs to let their hair down and show off their senses of humor while connecting with the American people on a human level.

The HBO sitcom *Veep* (2012-) also satirizes the American government, but it does not give politicians the type of direct voice they find on other series, despite the claim of many D.C. insiders claim the show is actually quite an accurate depiction of Washington. Show runner Armando Iannucci reportedly turns down politicians who have requested to be on the show because it would raise too many questions. The writers' only aim for the series is to make fun of politicians, especially the ones who watch the show and refuse to believe they are the butt of the joke ("D.C. Insiders Call *Veep* the Most Realistic Show About Politics" 2014). Writers also play with issues of race, gender, and foreign relations on the series because there is no way to rightfully avoid them, but these hot button issues are mere buttresses to the show's overall message: American politicians survive on contradictions to create the illusion that they long to serve the greater American public when, in truth, their greatest concern is their personal success. American nationalism leads viewers to believe politicians should be loyal to their constituents before anyone and anything else. They *should* be willing to make any sacrifice for the betterment of American citizens and to pursue government positions because they feel a calling to do so, not because officials feel it will benefit them personally, especially monetarily. In actuality, this is not the case, which makes *Veep* a surprisingly authentic portrayal of that political reality.

In the HBO sitcom *Veep*, Selina Meyer (Julia Louis-Dreyfus) is the Vice President of the United States, a position supposedly focused more on service than navigating political power. Selina tries to maintain a dignified reputation despite constant reminders that she is only the President's substitute. Her incompetent staff is incapable of accomplishing pretty much every task she assigns while their obliviousness only insinuates her more deeply into difficult situations. Selina perpetuates a culture of sarcasm and swearing during her furious fits when incompetent members of her staff are obviously trying to hide their inferiority. For example, in the episode "Full Disclosure," Selina threatens to fire someone from her staff whom she calls "non-fucking-functional." She stands over the staffer, who sits on a couch looking down at the ground, and goes on to blame the employee for her continuously low approval ratings, although she has no idea how to raise them either. As a political satire, one would expect that *Veep* would be ready to tackle many of the current political issues – race, feminism, gay marriage, etc. – head on, but the stakes turn out to be considerably lower in the scheme of things. The show is not meant to satirize political issues per se; instead, it targets politicians who are supposed to know how to handle them but do not. *Veep* suggests that politicians are normal people suffering from imposter syndrome, and that they are people who do not care for political correctness, American ideals, or the general public, a depiction that contrasts with popular expectations of American politicians. Although the show does not include cameo appearances by real politicians, there are obvious parallels between *Veep* and America's current political climate, similarities that set the show up as a primer for understanding president-elect Donald Trump.

The biggest difference between Selina Meyer and Donald Trump is that one lost a presidential election and the other did not. On second thought, another contrast is that Selina sets all of her hopes and dreams on the presidency while Donald* seemingly won it on a whim, as if his foray into politics were a new hobby that just happened to work out well for him. Other than that and their private parts (I think), Selina might as well be the female version of Donald – narcissistic, intellectually dull, ditsy, and perverse. They both deny outside characterizations of them as racists who love being the center of attention and use other people to their benefit. During the second season of the series, Selina's daughter, Catherine (Sarah Sutherland), wants her mother to meet her Middle Eastern boyfriend – a conversation that happens via Skype because Selina is too busy maintaining her public image and Catherine is usually deemed a distraction. In frustration, Catherine implies that her mother is racist to which Selina replies, "Okay, Catherine, you know that I am not a racist. My boyfriend in college was a quarter Cherokee, so…" President Trump's romantic relationships with international women, including his current wife Melania Trump, also serve to excuse his racist remarks against African Americans and immigrants, such as his claims that black people are surrounded by failure and that Mexicans are rapists.

Sexual deviance is a quality Selina and Donald can only see in others and not themselves. During a visit to Finland for trade negotiations, Selina enjoys a smoke with Osmo Häkkinen (Dave Foley), the Prime Minister's husband, and he grabs her breast. Selina, in shock, finds Gary (Anthony "Tony" Hale), her personal aide, and tells him about the incident, "I'm the Vice President of the United States, and he just squeezed my boob." The scene does

---

* In the original draft of this chapter, I referred to them as "Selina" and "President Trump" but elected to use parallel designations to avoid reinforcing gender inequality.

not work to address sexual assault against women because her disbelief at Osmo grabbing her breast is not attributed to the fact that she is a woman but to her individual status as a high-ranking official. Instead, the scene suggests that only individuals who hold the most esteemed positions are permitted to commit disrespectful acts. In Selina's mind, she should have been the assaulter, not the assaulted – an idea perpetuated by her statement in "New Hampshire" when she acts as the sitting president after the actual president resigns, "God, I would love to fuck a firefighter. Hey, I'm the president. I can fuck anybody I want now, right?"

Donald seems to feel that way, too. According to a vulgar conversation recorded in 2005, he talked about groping, kissing, and attempting to have sex with desirable women when he said, "When you're a star, they let you do it" (Fahrentold, "Trump recorded having extremely lewd conversation"). When five teenagers of color – four African Americans and one Hispanic – were accused of raping a white, female jogger, however, he demanded that the death penalty be reinstated to punish them. Donald purchased an ad in *The New York Times* that read: "They must serve as examples so that others will think long and hard before committing a crime or an act of violence" (Laughland, "Donald Trump and the Central Park Five"). Evidence later proved that the boys were wrongly convicted, but the President has reiterated rather than walked back his statements about their guilt while maintaining a double standard regarding his own behavior. Apparently, Donald does not consider grabbing women's pussies a crime when he is the perpetrator. To him, when you are powerful, "You can do anything." Selina's dialogue and hypocritical attitudes toward other people who exhibit the same perverse behavior reflects that idea: status trumps (pun intended) punishment.

In addition to sexual language, neither Selina nor Donald is afraid to drop the f-bomb as Donald did at a rally in New Hampshire. Ubiquitous cursing in *Veep* may surprise first-time viewers. Yet, the coarse language represents politicians' apathy toward political correctness and highlights their artificiality. All political characters on the show use vulgar language to express themselves, especially in high-pressure situations. For example, when Amy (Anna Clumsky), Selina's problem-solver (Chief of Staff and later Campaign Manager), signs her own name instead of Selina's signature on a condolence card, Selina comes out of her office in the middle of a meeting and curses her out. In this scene, cursing is used to illustrate a power shift. Amy does not curse at all and barely even speaks in this scene, which demonstrates her inferior position. When Selina returns to her "official meeting" in her office, the Vice President omits swear words from her vocabulary, raises her voice an octave, and resumes her meeting with a smile. Cursing, lashing out, and hurling insults at subordinates exhibits domination while the absence of vulgarity in other scenes suggests inauthenticity and politicians' phoniness in public spaces.

Series writers appropriate a faux feminism to amplify politicians' fakeness by having female characters curse on the show. Swearing is often viewed as "unladylike" behavior, and there are many times when Selina swears at her team as a strategy for reinforcing her power. Cursing in other situations is used to portray panic or disorganization, however. Therefore, cursing only humanizes Selina instead of functioning to dismantle gender norms. It makes her more authentic, which also makes her more likeable to viewers – the same process America is witnessing with Donald. His authenticity is new and refreshing for some Americans who aren't convinced that civilized, honest, and eligible politicians exist. As a female inhabiting a position of power, Selina has to navigate her femininity carefully to appear capable at all times. She makes it clear to her staff that she holds the power in every situation, especially with Gary Walsh (Tony Hale), the loyal secretary whose main job is to carry everything for her (hand sanitizer, tissue, and even tampons). Although Selina bosses her subordinates around, she relies on them for political strategies because she is often too ditsy to answer questions intelligently and make decisions. They are continuously scrambling to make sure she does not say or do anything that could debunk her political image, just as Donald's team has periodically banned him from Twitter. To ensure her success, Gary follows her around and whispers information in her ear to aid in her interactions with other government officials, military personnel, and professional sports teams.

Truthfully, the Vice President's Director of Communications, Dan Egan (Reid Scott), is fully in charge of her decision-making and, like advisers to Donald Trump, he urges Selina to skate around policy. For example, she is forced to improvise during one of her speeches because the President orders his messenger Jonah Ryan (Timothy Simons), to make adjustments to her speech. His "adjustments" actually involve scratching out the entire thing. As Selina is giving the speech, the camera zooms in on her notecards, which are completely obliterated. She makes remarks that parallel Donald's answers to debate questions as she states, "Politics is about people, it's about people," and a man in the crowd shouts out, "Is your guy going to be tweeting about this?" This is a hilarious remark because anyone who knows anything about Donald is aware of his Twitter obsession, and this comment from the crowd is a jab at Donald's ability to say more words in a tweet than he can string together in any sentence spoken out loud.

Many Americans watched the 2016 election results in shock as state after state turned red on the electoral map. An election centered more on low human morale than on public policy revealed where integrity ranked on America's list of qualities for a viable presidential candidate. After Donald's election, more and more of his supporters unveiled their loyalty for the businessman. *Veep's* loyal staffer Gary is emblematic of the silent supporter phenomenon that resulted in false predictions of a Hillary Clinton victory by landslide. Gary is the archetype of a "Trump supporter" in that he stands by Selina no matter what she says or does. He never stands less than two feet from her, and when she is upset, he goes to great lengths to comfort her, whether that requires rubbing her shoulder or fetching her desserts from all over Washington. Gary is like silent "Trump supporters" because no one pays attention to him, and he does not bring attention to himself. Many people consider him unintelligent, and he is considered the laughingstock. In rare moments when Selina is actually victorious, however, he is elevated and can share in her triumph because he is the only one who truly believes in her.

Viewers know Gary gets frustrated with Selina at times, but he never shows his anger toward her until "East Wing," an episode in the fourth season when he lashes out at Selina after she calls him "unimportant." He yells, "I have broken my back for you! I have let myself be laughed at! I have let myself be humiliated! And I'm happy to do it! Most of the time, you don't even know that I exist, but I am fucking everything to you!" Even after the argument, Gary comforts Selina with a "light, spongy" cake that he has ready for the occasion. The argument sheds light on Donald's relationship with his supporters. We have not heard him say it yet, but it is likely he deems them "unimportant" even though he would not have won the presidency if it were not for their support. The big question, of course, is whether or not his supporters will finally lash out at him if Donald does not keep his promises over the next four years? If *Veep* is a completely accurate representation of politics, then it does not matter. His supporters will continue to support him in the end.

Another similarity between Selina and Donald is their ability to manipulate gender norms to win over a crowd. Selina cries while Donald exhibits anger and refuses to cry. In the episode "Tears," congressman Roger Furlong (Dan Bakkedahl) asks Selina not to endorse him for governor of Ohio because her approval ratings are embarrassingly low. She begins to cry during a talk with the governor, which sparks an idea for Mike and Amy to pursue later. Mike McLintock (Matt Walsh) and Amy try to get her to cry again during an interview with a reporter to gain sympathy from her audience and, thus, boost her approval ratings. Selina attributes her tears to her exhaustion from being on "duty" 24/7. She quickly relates her feelings to the people of Ohio and how tired they must be, a move that turns out to be fortuitous in the end. Selina's crying scene may be reminiscent of Hillary Clinton's emotional moment in 2008 in New Hampshire. As Rebecca Curnalia and Dorian Mermer argue, female political candidates have to walk a fine line between femininity and masculinity to gain favor with the public, a concept they refer to as a "gender double bind" (27). Selina demonstrates, however, that the public actually wants to see the very side of a man or a woman that conventional wisdom suggests makes them incapable of holding positions of power – their emotions. For Donald, the dominant emotion is anger.

During several debates and interviews, Donald's red face gets redder, he raises his voice, and he refuses to let others speak. Many politicians and journalists claim that Donald has an anger problem, but his success argues otherwise. In several interviews and speeches, he strategically directs his anger toward the government while arguing that it is not running the country properly, a move that works for him because many Americans are able to relate to being angry with the government. In another interview with Christian Broadcasting Network's David Brody, Donald explains that he does not cry because he does not have time. Donald differs from Selina in this regard (if what he is says is true), but he is like her in that he confirms it is okay to cry. He states, "I know plenty of people that cry. They're good people" ("Donald Trump's Amazing Answer to 'Do You Cry?'") For Donald, all emotions are appropriate – he simply chooses anger.

Selina and Donald's political play with emotions illustrates that gender norms are social constructions and serve as another playground of opportunity for politicians to gain traction with the public. According to Jessica Birthisel and Jason Martin (64), the sitcom *The Office* (2005-2013) also relies on gender norms, stereotypes, and corporate codes of behavior and management within an office space to perform satire. They argue the show's satire is successful in mocking patriarchal authority and hegemonic masculinity through its production style and exaggeration. Nonetheless, the lack of repercussions for offending characters and stereotypical portrayals of women in the workplace undermines the transgressive potential of the series. *Veep* almost does the opposite. The series disrupts and completely dismantles gender stereotypes because, in the first place, they do not hold true and, in the second place, can be performed. If gender norms were correct guidelines for success, then Selina's approval ratings would have dropped after her constant crying, and Donald would have lost the election.

Selina and Donald's popularity with the people also overcomes their obvious difficulty answering complex questions about foreign policy (or any actual policy for that matter) and their rambling, inelegant speeches. Both politicians are guilty of several gaffes that show attempts to cover up their lack of knowledge on a subject. During a visit to a U.S. Marine base, Selina is going down the line and shaking hands with marines while Gary follows behind her whispering information about each marine in her ear as is their routine. As she reaches one marine, Gary informs her that he is a mortarman, or a soldier who operates a firing device. Selina blankly smiles at the Marine and says, "Oh, a mortarman. That means there's mortar-you than meets the eye." In her speech during her short time as Commander-in-Chief after the president resigns, her team has technical difficulties with the teleprompter, and Selina is forced to improvise, which is not her greatest strength. She begins to dance around policy statements with meaningless metaphors comparing the future to a train and asking Americans to "meet me at the station." Once the teleprompter is fixed, her team celebrates only to realize that the revised speech still has the previous president's spending plan in it. Selina begins to read the speech word for word – an allusion to Melania Trump's plagiarized speech delivered at the Republican National Convention.

Donald, too, stumbled over his words when NBC's Chuck Todd asked him who inspired him in terms of foreign policy. Donald replied, "Well, I really watch the shows. You really see a lot of great, you know, when you watch your show and all of the other shows, and you have the generals and you have certain people that you like" before going on to name former United Nations Ambassador John Bolton and Jack Jacobs, a retired colonel in the United States Army (who claimed he had hardly spoken with the candidate). It is hard to say which among his slip-ups is the worst. Some might argue his mistake of referring to 9/11 as 7-eleven is the worst, but perhaps calling Iraq the "Harvard for terrorism" when he praised Saddam Hussein for killing terrorists "so good" is worse. Even when Donald admits his absurdity, he ends up looking even more ridiculous. For instance, the time he was asked about the endorsement from the Ku Klux Klan, he responded, "Well, just so you understand, I don't know anything about David Duke, okay? I don't know anything about what you're even talking about with white supremacy or white supremacists. So, I don't know." This even though his white privilege is apparent in his quote, ""It has not been easy for me ... My father gave me a small loan of a million dollars" ("The 37 Fatal Gaffes That Didn't Kill Donald Trump"). Both Donald and Selina are guilty of fallacies and stringing together sentences that make no logical sense as if they are trying to say everything to cover all the bases without saying anything at all.

Another area of struggle for both Donald and Selina is their relationships with foreign countries. Selina attends the White House Correspondents' Dinner where she performs a song that is initially a big hit until it backfires. In preparation for the dinner, Selina suggests her team come up with a song making fun of the new Speaker of the House to make a humorous reference to her party being wiped out in the election. But, upon realizing that the idea might result in the Speaker of the House getting offended and taking out his anger on her in federal budget negotiations, they decide instead to do a parody of "50 Ways to Leave your Lover," a classic song by American, singer-songwriter Paul Simon. Her song, "50 Ways to Win Denver," takes several jabs at the White House and at politicians who make promises they can't keep and put on acts to win over the public. Unfortunately for Selina, though, her lines "Don't be European, Ian/Say 'screw France,' Lance/Maybe the Germans, Herman/The Dutch, the Swedes," offend European leaders. As result, she travels to Europe to make apologies to save her reputation and mend foreign relationships. Donald is less apologetic about promises to build a wall between Mexico and the United States to prevent illegal immigration. During his statements, he offends the Mexican people when he describes them as drug dealers and racists. He says, "When Mexico sends its people, they're not sending their best. They're not sending you. They're not sending you. They're sending people that have lots of problems, and they're bringing those problems with us. They're bringing drugs. They're bringing crime. They're rapists. And some, I assume, are good people." Yet, he promised during his campaign that funding for the wall would come from the Mexican government, a plan most people found ridiculous, as common etiquette would advise against insulting someone before you asking for something. Since his election, he has shown attempts to make nice with Mexicans and Mexican Americans by calling them "amazing people." Neither Selina nor Donald shows general concern for groups of people. Instead, people are little more than political pawns to be used for their benefit.

Not only do Selina and Donald not care about different groups of people, they also have a categorical disregard for individuals, too, ranging from certain politicians to some of their own offspring. Donald is noted as saying he is proud of all of his children except for one, Tiffany Trump, whom he is proud of but to a "lesser extent" than the others. His reason for being less proud of her is because she just got out of school and, therefore, has not been as involved with his businesses or political campaigns. For most of the series, Selina's daughter Catherine is a background character. Her mother only pays attention to her when Catherine causes a public relations crisis for Selina, like the time she writes a college essay that contradicts Selina's beliefs on foreign policy with Israel. At one point, Selina and Catherine are getting their hair done, and Selina tells the hairdresser to make sure to give Catherine's hair a lot of volume because her skull is "kind of indented." Additionally, Catherine has to make appointments to spend time with her mother, and she is treated like any other person Selina has on her schedule during these meetings, as Gary follows behind the Vice President and gives her updates on her own daughter's life (basic information such as when she gets a new roommate or is working on a new assignment for school). Ironically, Catherine knows her mother better than anyone else and is like her in many ways. She is the only one who is not afraid to call her out on her stupidity, but she does not do so in ways that could damage her mother's political reputation. One of the first times Catherine appears on the show, she reveals that Mike's dog, which he uses as an excuse to leave work early and get out of after-hours office events, is actually fake. Selina is the only person on the series who does not know this in advance of the revelation. Like Catherine, Donald's children are also loyal to him. In interviews, they resist giving answers that will deprecate their father and are heavily involved in his political and business affairs.

Overall, the similarities between Selina and Donald are astounding only because there is such a high expectation for politicians to be honest, candid, and have some understanding of how the American government works. Ironically, those misconceptions are exactly why the show succeeds. Selina and her staff's inappropriate behavior, vulgar language, lack of preparation, and disorganization are all unexpected elements that contradict public perceptions of government officials. Nonetheless, parallels between the show and real-life politicians suggest that *Veep is* a precise portrayal of political life in America. The irony of the show is its absence of irony. With Trump as our President, *Veep* becomes even more real than before imagined. America does not have to resort to *Veep* to watch a president strapped with insults ready to fire at any moment, listen to constant cursing and off-hand remarks that may or may not be offensive (depending on who you are), and laugh at awkward encounters between a politician who answers questions by avoiding them. All viewers have to do is to tune in to the news. The show's aesthetic similarity to *The Office* – also filmed with a single-camera following the characters in mockumentary style and the dull backdrops and under-saturated colors that make the scenery mundane – provides a subtle, yet strategic, reminder that the White House is not a marvelous mansion, as it may seem to members of the public, but it is a workplace like any other office. Officials and staffers go to work, do what they need to do, and try to get off early if they can, just like the rest of us. Also, the issues that Selina and her associates deal with humanize them and show viewers that these elites are really just like normal people. For instance, Selina has digestion issues at a frozen yogurt shop in "Frozen Yoghurt," and her staff tries to shove her back in the limo unnoticed as reporters are taking pictures of her.

Veep is hilarious, fun, and provides what used to be a refreshing parody of the current political climate, but what was once refreshing may be more accurate now than the general public realizes. The underlying message of the show is important because it is a wake-up call to viewers to remember that politicians are people, too, and citizens should not be fooled by leaders' fancy suits and political jargon. Officials run to the bathroom and curse when they stub their toes exactly like the rest of us. Just as we scrutinize celebrities in the entertainment field (and it certainly seems lines between politics and entertainment are blurring), we criticize politicians and expect them to uphold a certain standard at all times. Is this a realistic expectation for our politicians? How much impact does our attention have on what they reveal and what they hide? What qualities do we *really* look for in a candidate? The parallels between *Veep* and real-world politics – for example, the episode "Tears," which is perceived to be a mockery of Hillary Clinton's becoming emotional on the campaign trail – are obvious signs that the writers are making fun of the hypocrisy in America's political climate. The series plays off of common public distrust of politicians and satirizes the way people imagine politicians behave in real life. Ironically, it is extremely probable that the writers are not far off the mark. On the one hand, the similarities between the show and the current state of the American government is disheartening because it is a reflection of a society that votes for political leaders based on image rather than their intellectual abilities and the true belief that a candidate is capable of running a country. This pattern of representation demonstrates that some citizens gravitate toward rhetoric based on what they want to hear instead of digging more deeply into the content and context of what is actually being said by the candidates. This duality between what is appearance and what is substance shows America is a country that lacks concern for education, credibility, and respect among elected politicians, which shows it must not be the standard to which we hold for ourselves. Finally, it is discouraging to find this proof that those who play by the rules, even when the rules are unfair, will lose. The silver lining is that *anyone really can* become President.

WE'RE ALL IN THIS SICK, SAD WORLD TOGETHER
(I GUESS)

Elyse Conklin

Who are you and why are you reading my chapter? No…that came out wrong….don't go, don't take that the wrong way…take it as an invitation. Who are you and why are you reading my chapter? Well, while I have your attention, let's talk about me for a minute. Do you remember the meme "describe yourself in three fictional characters?" For a couple weeks it was all over my Facebook and Twitter feeds. A self-deprecating or self-aggrandizing way to direct the conversation toward yourself, your taste, personality, and generate an insight on self-definition vs. social perception, depending on whether the virtual Greek chorus agreed or disagreed. [I'm a bit cynical about these like-baits.] So naturally I would start with Daria Morgendorffer. But I've also been told I'm more of a Jane, somehow even more sardonic and misanthropic. I can't help myself…I grew up in the same suburban enclave depicted in the movie Mean Girls, *but when Daria aired from 1997-2002, I was in middle school awkwardly listening to the Strokes and reading* A Tree Grows in Brooklyn *by myself during the lunch hours. Of course, and please don't let this get around, I also played Mariah Carey's #1s cassette and Britney Spears on repeat. I still think Toxic is the greatest song ever made. Shhhh….So I think April Lundgate rounds this out. She's basically Daria as an adult who secretly loves puppies. Ugh, I swear, I normally don't post these kinds of things.*

 elyzus

describe yourself in three fictional characters

4.1 Tracy Grandstaff as Daria Morgendroffer, (upper right) Wendy Hoopes as Jane Lane, (lower right) in Daria, "Fire!" Aubrey Plaza as April Lundgate in Parks and Recreation, "The Wall"

The specular meme demands: describe yourself in three fictional characters. *The meme demands a cultural self-portrait. Who do you see yourself in and does your audience of followers agree?*

This chapter proceeds from and builds upon the Althusserian and Lacanian theoretical foundation regarding the constitution of the subject through language and institutions. I begin with the argument that the sitcom serves as a technology within the televisual apparatus as a mode of interpolation. In occupying the role of critic, I intend to work through the "task of rhetorical construction – the temporary fixing and stabilizing of discourse to reveal its location in social space and relations of power" (Cloud 150). The trend of association and identification within the fictional character meme demonstrates how materialist pop culture functions as both a mirror for the desires of public consumption and as the driving force behind production. As a certain someone would say, "the map precedes the territory" (Baudrillard "Simulation" 166).

As a ubiquitous method of sociocultural construction and consumption, fictional television propels innovation and shapes the behaviors and attitudes of its market (Kellner 231). Networks produce content designed to be appealing enough for audiences to seek it out; concurrently, the discerning public develops its personal taste for products through an affective relationship with programming. Building on Barthe's notion of textual mediation, Ann Kaplan describes "the fictive text as necessarily constructing the subject in the processes of reception" (Kaplan 25). Subject formation and cultural consumption are intimately tied; Sitcoms, like memes, mediate and reflect "'micropolitical' worlds of identity, relationship, consumption" (Johnson 38).

If we accept Douglas Kellner's definition of contemporary identity as a series of "social constructs, arbitrary notions which serve to mark and call attention to certain phenomena and which fulfill certain analytical or classificatory tasks" for the purpose of self-presentation in our worldly interactions, then any coherent phenomenological study must explore the relational contours of pop culture (Kellner 259). Brian L. Ott clarifies: "...television furnishes consumers with explicit identity models, models not of who to be but how to be. Viewers learn to fashion their identities by watching popular characters fashion theirs. Second, television furnishes consumers with the symbolic resources – the actual cultural bricks – with which to (re)construct identity. Viewers continuously construct and deconstruct their identities from those bricks. Thus, television both shapes the nature of identity by providing identity models and provides the symbolic resources for enactment. (Ott 58)

This chapter proceeds from and aims to build on a rich canon of cultural studies through an analysis of the relationship between production and identity construction in the context of the animated MTV sitcom *Daria*. In both its form and content, the textual terrain of *Daria* demonstrates the tension of identity development from the perspective of a suburban teenage girl in order to illuminate the "sense of betweenness" characteristic of contemporary identity (Kellner 49). Much like the audience of MTV, Daria Morgendorffer exists in the liminal space between childhood dependence on the tantalizing cusp of adulthood – "not a girl, not yet a woman" (I told you, I love Britney Spears). As an alienated cynical teenager, Daria operates as a transgressive cultural obstruction to the "truth" of suburban life; working through moments and tropes of the show reveals the model of wish fulfillment embedded within the simulation MTV tries to create and the real it is trying to describe. Through the use of "accommodational cynicism" *Daria* ultimately begs the question – what does it mean to resist, and is it futile?

What Sitcoms Reveal

Starting from the premise that cultural institutions reflect and generate markers of identity and subjectivity, the development of the modern sitcom toward postmodernity similarly parallels larger sociocultural trends in the realm of the simulacra. In the advent of the sitcom, Kellner characterizes modern identity as centered around "one's function in the public sphere (or family)...fundamental choices that defined who one was (profession, family, political identification, and so on)" (Kellner 242). Take the earliest forms of sitcom in *Leave it to Beaver*: the characters are one-dimensional. June Cleaver is defined exclusively by her representation of the perfect mother/wife figure. Sitcoms from this era lack layers and complexity; the characters function as empty vessels to fill in the role of the idealized subject. "Objectively, we know that the Cleavers represent an ideal rather than a norm, and that confines and constricts individuality. Emotionally, though, we cannot escape the sense that life would be much better if our lives were just like the Cleavers' lives" (Kutulas 17). In a Lacanian sense, this era of television evokes the mirror-phase; one-note characters operate as a symbolic representation of identity perfection.

The rise and proliferation of sitcom programming coincides with the evolution of global Post-Fordist capitalism and the loss of spatial and familial stability. A cultural shift took place in the late sixties, a form of global awareness made possible through the creation of an international theaters – for example, the way the Vietnam War could be broadcast to televisions across the world in American living rooms. Individuals were no longer anchored to their locality or reliant upon their immediate family or community for cultural stimulation. Ott describes this process on both a global and local level: when "the economic mode shifts from a goods-based model to a service-based one, from centralized

53

mass production to transnational, global culture industries, subjects are less able to locate their identities in pre-given categories and ascribed roles" (Ott 57).

As globalization and the growth of liquid capital rendered borders and origins functionally meaningless in terms of production and consumption, individuals and subjectivity congruently entered the realm of deterritorialization. Gilles Deleuze and Félix Guattari explain how the dissemination of images, signs, and culture through sitcoms onto the subject contribute to this process:

> These images do not initiate a making public of the private so much as a privatization of the public: the whole world unfolds right at home, without one's having to leave the TV screen. This gives private persons a very special role in the system: a role of *application*, and no longer of *implication*, in a code.
> (Deleuze and Guattari 251)

The development and perfection of industry meant that basic needs could not only be easily met through purchase, but also infinitely customizable. A surplus always exists in normal life, the foundation of Maslow's hierarchy of needs for the average postmodern citizen-subject is always met, changing the nature of what it means to desire. For example, take the way grocery stores maintain stock far beyond what would ever be sold in an average week. Those who rely upon that grocery to survive never fear walking in with a full wallet and leaving empty-handed. Instead, they only risk purchasing something that will make them unhappy. The proliferation of goods and choices means we no longer have to direct our desire toward filling our basic needs – there will always be enough bread in the capitalist machine. Desire is now the drive to produce, to *apply* what we internalize from television and other state apparatuses (Deleuze and Guattari 256). Rather than "let them eat cake!" postmodernity asks, "would you like devil's food or Funfetti?"

In a micropolitical sense, the shift in the meaning of desire serves to complicate the relationship between culture and identity, creating a sense of power over self-presentation. We no longer see our favorite characters as an ideal to strive for, instead our attachment "occupies the individual as subject in the terms of the existing social representations and it constructs the individual as subject in the process, in the balancing out of symbolic and imaginary, circulation for fixity" (Heath, 127). Culture has become self-constitutive through the intertextuality of the production, distribution, and consumption of media.

Describe yourself in three fictional characters.

Until this point, it appears as though the process of identity construction in postmodern culture is one of awareness and choice. Aesthetics, brands, style, and other forms of identity markers stem from a conscious decision to take on what feels authentic; because subjectivity is no longer defined by static orientations, a sense of malleable reflexivity as well as a wider array of choices enables individuals to determine their sense of self (Kellner 243). In an Althusserian sense, the superstructure of global capitalism determines the direction of politics and history toward accumulation and growth of the State on a macrolevel. On a microlevel, ideology sustains the raison d'etre of the State by turning individuals in subjects through "a representation of the imaginary relationship of individuals to their real conditions of existence" (Althusser 162). "Ideological State Apparatuses" such as school and church instill the desire for recognition and inclusion within civil society; the televisual apparatus provides "a tactic of potentialities linked to usage....for mastery, control and command, an optimization of the play of possibilities" for identity formation

(Baudrillard "Ecstasy" 127). In the realm of the material, the subject has become merely the "interface" between capitalist production and the commodity; the landscape of banality in advanced capitalism gives way to the "projective, imaginary and symbolic" realm of the television (Baudrillard "Ecstasy" 126).

Daria as a Cultural Text

   In response to a burgeoning sense of globalization, Daria Morgendorffer emerged the toneless voice of a listless and alienated youth as the 20th century drew to a close. *Daria* left a significant mark on pop culture through her bitingly sardonic nature and the presence of ironic cultural commentary throughout the show's five season run from 1997- 2002. The overarching programming strategy of MTV during this time period was in flux, moving away from exclusively music video content and toward the "real" MTV with shows like *The Real World* and *Beavis and Butthead*. MTV uniquely blurs the lines between the "categories of ads and programs, it emphasizes the fragmentary nature of all things..." (Rabinovitz 100), which begs a cultural "chicken or egg" question regarding the form of MTV and its content: are the music videos, TV shows, and commercials, being played because they reflect the tastes of the audience or because corporate sponsors have determined it is most likely to appeal to what audiences think their desires are?

   The following section utilizes the method of cultural materialism in order to situate *Daria* as an object of analysis within the system of postmodern media communication. Ann Kaplan describes the role of critical theory to "expose how these practices posing as speaking what is "natural" and "true," in fact set up a transcendental self as a point outside articulation" (Kaplan 147). As a cultural artifact, *Daria* reflects the contradiction of resistance, pleasure, and complicity inherent in postmodern identity while utilizing "more direct forms of risky truth-telling at her disposal as she aims at the transformed care of self" (Salvato 150).

Daria came into existence with the purpose of elevating the intellectual content of MTV programming (especially compared to *Beavis and Butthead*) while appealing to new, female audiences as "a girl hit!" The creator explains that, as a character, Daria developed from the cultural milieu, taking snippets from Janeane Garofalo on *The Ben Stiller Show* and Sara Gilbert's Darlene Conner character from *Roseanne*. She was supposed to be "pretty and plain," simple, but not ugly (Andrews). *Daria* represented a countercultural cynic produced from the heart of corporate production; an ironic, feminist hero encapsulating the "riot grrrrl" movement of the early '90s with the purpose of creating and integrating uncharted audience territory through a narrative of teenage resilience. In a Foucauldian sense, the power that created Daria was a productive parsing together of cultural fragments, resulting in a text where reality and fiction coalesce (Baudrillard "Ecstacy" 126).

A spin-off of MTV's *Beavis and Butthead*, *Daria* echoes the countercultural skepticism and alienation emblematic of her origins. Kellner characterizes *Beavis and Butthead* as a "subversive" criticism of MTV itself through depictions of their alienation from pop culture and the typical ambitions of modern life. *Beavis and Butthead* signifies the all-consuming force of pop media; as characters, they "get all of their ideas and images concerning life from the media and their entire view of history and the world is entirely derived from media culture....with a sense of no future" (Kellner 145). Viewers were drawn to the anger, frustration, and meaninglessness of the nihilistic characters but insulated through a sense of safe yet ironic relatability. Individuals could consume music videos through the show before *Beavis and Butthead* came on and then laugh along with the characters as they mocked the same music videos played 20 minutes earlier. Daria shares the disdain for the banality of suburban life emblematic of *Beavis and Butthead*, but instead she infiltrates civil society, as opposed to the pessimistic destruction of her origins. Both shows offered audiences guilt-free pop culture consumption with an air of elevated detachment, a justification for going "mainstream" with a wink of self-awareness.

Daria begins with her move from one generic town to another. Lawndale is the terrain of normalcy where her boring corporate parents stress over work while her boring beauty queen sister obsesses over popularity and clothes. Daria's flat cynicism serves as the "antagonism to the system" in order to disrupt and refuse the smooth functioning of suburbia (Laclau and Mouffe 89). A standard episode of *Daria* links the narrative of conflict between Daria and the mainstream push of school culture by revealing how her cynicism and intelligence counters the hegemonic forces of popularity and stymies the school administrators. Nick Salvato defines her cynicism as a response to this sense of disdainful helplessness, "a melancholic, self-pitying reaction to the apparent disintegration of political reality" (Salavto 132). The opening theme song sequence demonstrates her resignation from school life; an expressionless Bartleby-esque Daria moves through daily life, present but effortless, as she barely waves at a volleyball in gym class after it has already bounced in front of her.

Daria is *in* her suburban nightmare of Lawndale but not *of* it. The pilot of *Daria* begins as the Morgendorffers family moves to a new, but still familiar, town. The first exchange of the series tells the audience Daria is different:

> Jake: Girls, I just want you to know your mother and I realize it's not easy moving to a whole new town -- especially for you, Daria, right?
>
> Daria: Did we move?

Jake: (laughs) I'm just saying you don't make friends as easily as... uh, some people.

Turns out, it's actually pretty easy to move when the dynamics of their previous social location play out in a predictable fashion: Daria's vapid and conventionally attractive sister Quinn instantly identifies with the popular Fashion Club as Daria settles into her familiar status as an outsider. Daria eschews mainstream trends through her trademark combat boots and glasses and subsequently finds sardonic solidarity in Jane (her multiple ear piercings, grungy outfit, and dry conversation style communicates the countercultural harmony between the two). Daria and Quinn's initiation to Lawndale demonstrates that place no longer matters in the context of the high school subjectivity; the act of "copy and paste" for the symbolic representations of each sibling produces the same social dynamic in a decentered suburbia. The diverging experiences of each sibling highlights the importance of identity construction in the realm of the social; given that their material relationship to the world is identical, the contrast between the two serves to delineate their symbolic differences.

Unpacking the episodes "Through a Lens Darkly" and "Quinn the Brain" establishes the comparative frame for the nature and implications of "user's choice" identity formation. In "Lens," Daria undergoes a temporary transformation by substituting her glasses for contacts while Quinn takes on the social position of "nerd" after stumbling into an accidentally brilliant English essay. Daria, in a conversation with her mother, initially resists the symbolic meaning behind the act of discarding her glasses:

Daria: We've   had   this
           conversation before. You
           think if I get contacts I'll

	suddenly turn into the homecoming queen.
Helen:	(exasperated) Daria, you can't possibly have some ethical issue with wearing contacts.
Daria:	How about thinking people should accept me for who I am without my having to change?
Helen:	Right! They should accept you for who you are: a complex and interesting young lady worth knowing, instead of seeing your glasses and jumping to some moronic conclusion based on ridiculous stereotypes and their own ignorance.

The interaction between Daria and her mother cleverly foregrounds the absurdity of the symbolic meaning behind her glasses. The material function of contacts makes driving safer for Daria, yet the symbolic act of wearing them compels people, particularly *boys*, to treat her differently. Eventually Daria feels like a fraud for her improved social status over a meaningless aesthetic, and returns to her "true" self.

"Quinn the Brain" poses an interesting exploration of the relationship between identity and authenticity. Threatened with the possibility of repeating the ninth grade, Quinn's last-ditch effort on "Academic Imprisonment" gains her notoriety as a "brain." The essay itself is not particularly profound, but it contains my favorite line: For the school is my prison, and its teachers my imprisoners. Like a hamster on one of those wheel things, school runs us around and around until we yearn for the food pellet, but only more homework awaits." When Quinn begins wearing a black turtleneck and beret, however, Daria decides to switch the roles and dress like Quinn in order to test where she fits in now that she is no longer the "brainy" Morgendorffer girl. Removing her glasses and wearing makeup and fashionable clothes instantly brings boys and adoration to her side – the content of the subject is irrelevant, only the form matters.

Small motifs throughout the series emphasize both the banality and intensity of suburban life. Every meal the Morgendorffers share at the family table is the same; the repetition of lasagna as family dinner is an odd quirk – their table remains devoid of the diversity promised by innovative capitalism. Similarly, the stress of working life on adults appears in nearly every episode of *Daria;* both of Daria's parents are reformed hippies-turned-corporate-workers who struggle with balancing work and personal life, as the public has bled into the private. The bulging eye of the rage-filled history teacher, the consistently profit-driven bumbling principal, and the humorously misandrist science teacher all point to the alienation of academic labor.

These referents blend the line between reality and fiction, communicating the false narrative of the suburban utopia created by modernity. The ubiquitous media motif *Sick, Sad World* hammers this point in to the audience through the notion of "spectacle." Every time a television set is turned on in *Daria*'s world, 'Sick, Sad World' announces a surreal news story. TONIGHT! ON "SICK, SAD WORLD":

- "What's that you're really stirring in your tea, honey or bee vomit? Animal secretions that make us say 'yum.'"
- "Are fish using our oceans as their own private toilet?"

- "A vision of Christ in a half-eaten candy bar? Talk about my sweet lord! The Immaculate Confection, next on 'Sick, Sad World.'"
- "What do those Supreme Court judges wear under their robes? Declassified government polaroids next, on 'Sick, Sad World.'"

Through "Sick, Sad World," the creators of *Daria* parody the spectacularization of society through the absurdity of the news stories; yet, on some level, these narratives hold some truth, even predictive power (see "9 Times Daria's 'Sick, Sad World' Predicted Your Newsfeed" on MTV.com). Larry Law explains:

We live in a spectacular society, that is, our whole life is surrounded by an immense   accumulation of spectacles. Things that were once directly lived are now lived by proxy.   Once   an experience is taken out of the real world it becomes a commodity. As a   commodity the spectacular is developed to the detriment of the real. It becomes a   substitute for experience. (Law 2)

"Sick, Sad World" represents the cultural mirror of media obsession with the display of the absurd in order to conceal the banality of "the real." Viewers are meant to internalize the parallels from "Sick, Sad World" to our own media spectacles and how we become infatuated and distracted from our mundane surroundings and powerlessness.

Concluding Thoughts and Navigation Tactics

While technologies of consumerism produced the show *Daria*, the characters provide a guide to navigate structures that over determine reality. It would be easy to criticize Daria's misanthropy as a defense mechanism for her complicity in the cultural hegemony of capitalism and materialism in suburban Lawndale through her enjoyment of class privilege and a comfortable suburban existence. Working from Baudrillard's definition of dissimulation: "to dissimulate is to feign not to have what one has" (Baudrillard "Simulation" 167), one could argue her outlook functions as a dissimulation of privilege, belonging, and outsider status. Daria's dark attitude is supposed to demonstrate her outside-ness relative to the popular kids, yet she lives in her large house, maintains occasionally friendly relationships with Brittany and Kevin, and has the benefits of suburban resource and educational privilege pushing her toward a bright future. Her choice in black clothing, Doc Martens, and tragic disposition only demonstrates the "excessive proliferation of signs of the real and the authentic" by allowing Daria to hold onto some modicum of choice while she feels trapped and resentful of their suburban prison (Auslander 208).

Nick Salvato characterizes Daria's navigation tactic through high school fondly, however:

Cynical accommodation to systems and structures whose navigation is inevitable, but in navigating which tactical accommodation need not become accommodationist strategy: a critical cynicism that works precisely to identify and defend against such accommodationism…(Salvato 22)

Daria's position as a teenage girl reflects the learned helplessness of those who desire sociopolitical change in the face of inescapable systems of power. As a high school student, Daria cannot feasibly exist or gain the skills she needs to escape without the temporary compromise of living through her suburban path to adult liberation. Similarly, social forces have made it nearly impossible to resist neoliberal capitalism without engaging in it on some level. Recognizing contradictions through cynicism functions as a form of "paradoxically generative" affect rather than falling into the trap of "the enlightened false consciousness of postmodernity" (Salvato 134; Sloterdijk 5).

The episode "Fizz Ed" demonstrates the generative elements of Daria's cynicism as obstruction. Lawndale High is in a financial crisis with outdated textbooks and learning materials. Eventually, even the football team can't afford proper practice gear, triggering Principal Li's concern. Principal Li purposefully holds the referendum on the advertising contract during the Super Bowl, and only Jane and Daria show up to question her decision:

Daria: This isn't about whether I like soda. It's about whether a public high school should be using its status as a place of authority to serve as one more marketing tentacle of corporate America. With the taxpayers subsidizing it. This whole thing sucks. They shouldn't be selling stuff to people under the guise of educating them. Don't you think it's totally unethical and underhanded?

She makes a great point, so naturally Principal Li signs the contract anyway (cue commercial break). Daria speaks her truth as a method to at least refuse and impede the system. Daria's voice of reason ultimately wins out when the soda experiment cues the breakdown of all school functionality. Let the system destroy itself. Daria represents the counterpoint to what Lauren Berlant identifies as "cruel optimism," a subjective trap of modernity:

o Whatever the *experience* of optimism is in particular, then, the *affective structure*

o of an optimistic attachment involves a sustaining inclination to return

o to the scene of fantasy that enables you to expect that this time, nearness to

o this thing will help you or a world to become different in just the right way.

o But, again, optimism is cruel when the object/scene that ignites a sense of

o possibility actually makes it impossible to attain the expansive transformation

o for which a person or a people risks striving; and, doubly, it is cruel insofar

o as the very pleasures of being inside a relation have become sustaining

o regardless of the content of the relation, such that a person or a world finds

o itself bound to a situation of profound threat that is, at the same time, profoundly

o confirming. (Berlant 2)

Daria utilizes her method of flat, disaffected "risky truth-telling" as a form of "transformed care of self" while acknowledging the futility of her speaking truth to power (Salvato 150). Rather than expecting some form of radical awakening and change from the administration or her peers, she bides her time and exhausts the system through her accommodational cynicism. What else is there to do when political activism is rendered an empty and meaningless symbolic gesture? Postmodernity is now collapsing in on itself. The "reality television President" in power was elected without the popular majority despite the promise of liberalism to "get out and vote" as a form of progressive civic duty. Radical responses through protest have become an ad campaign, "The revolution will be televised – drink Pepsi!" The fantasy of liberal democracy unravels. Whatever.

[Edgy]

To jon sharp: for teaching me what it means to live amor fati *without giving up misanthropy.*

SHAMELESS APPAREL

Jenn St Sume

5.1 Ethan Cutkosky as Carl Gallagher in Shameless, "I Only Miss Her When I'm Breathing"

From the time *Roseanne* debuted in the late 1980s through the mid-2010s, the constitution of the situation comedy has shifted toward comedy of perverse exploitation. I define the comedy of exploitation as a subgenre of television shows that both amplify and bastardize the voices of marginalized groups. *Roseanne*, which was broadcast from 1988 to 1997 on ABC, focuses on the complicated social and economic struggles of a family as the context for the series, but situations presented typically center on the eponymous character, a woman. The series deviates from the mythical television norm of the White, suburban, upwardly mobile, materialistic, functional family; instead, the cast features Roseanne (Roseanne Barr) and Dan Conner (John Goodman) as functional members of the lower-working class. The comedy of *Roseanne* stems from the couple's ultimate resistance to a system that exploits their class position for the benefit of nameless and faceless people at the upper ends of the American social class system. Instead of assuming guilt for not living the traditional, middle-class life typically depicted on American television, the members of this TV family bond over a shared opportunity to make their way.

In many ways, *Roseanne* started a new era of television. Before this sitcom, the majority of series in the domcom (domestic comedy) or family sitcom subgenre focused on problems that were materialistic and easily solvable in thirty-minute time slots (McCleland 165-176). These situations and conflicts are amplified to seem problematic for the character while viewers recognize that, in reality, these issues are trivial in comparison to other real-life problems. Also, these programs focus on the characters' journeys to resolve the problem at hand. By keeping the focus on a particular character or group of characters, any critical, sociopolitical context is situated in the background if present at all. In the exploitation era, we see a shift in the *purpose* of contextual elements. Instead of establishing a televisual space where a character (or set of characters) might find redemption, the set itself – most often the Conner's modest and messy living room in fictional Lanford, Illinois – acts a critique of the larger culture. The shift toward a comedy of exploitation capitalizes on the context of a situation to critique a larger narrative existing outside of the set, both the location for shooting and the television set.

There are ways in which the Showtime series *Shameless*, which is based on a British television series and transplanted to Chicago, recalls elements of *Roseanne* but casts them in a much harsher light. Episodes of the show first aired in 2011, and the series is still on the air as of the publication of this anthology. In this essay, I argue that the comedy-drama *Shameless* situates the violent abuse of resources as a form of comedic exploitation. Furthermore, I argue that the context of the show exploits the value of Blackness and classicism to uphold a sacrosanct vision of

Whiteness that is presented as consistently fit to make the choices necessary to survive. I offer a Burkean analysis as the critical framework for examining how the context of the show functions to perpetuate capitalistic values. Throughout the chapter, I explore the use of class and race in *Shameless* to demonstrate a pervasive exploitation of particular voices in the name of comedy and with a discussion of the harmfulness of television's genre of exploitation.

Dramatism

Comedic exploitation focuses both on a character's use of agency *and* the context that creates the problem that is the locus for particular narratives. Kenneth Burke's theory of dramaticism offers a useful framework for understanding the relationship between a character and the larger context in a situation comedy. Within this scope, the context is the "scene," to use Burke's terminology, and this scene constitutes not only the material situation – the location, time, space, etc. – but the immaterial as well. In television, we refer to these contextual places as the scenario of a given plot. A scenario encompasses the fictional space a character inhabits as well as the collective cultural, moral, and ethical beliefs through which that space is constructed. The ability of characters to create meaningful relationships, reason through challenges, solve problems, and the like is then defined as their agency or the *means* through which an actor chooses to operate in response to the scenario. In sum, a character in a situation comedy can then be seen as the actor who operates within the scenario to achieve a particular goal (Burke 152-6).

In *Shameless*, the setting is a poverty-ridden, gang-infused, neighborhood of Southside Chicago. The show focuses on the Gallaghers, a family of seven unorthodox characters featured regularly and other family members who figure into the story peripherally or drop into the narrative on occasion. Fiona

Gallagher (Emmy Rossum), the eldest daughter of the bunch, functions as the matriarch (viewers learn that the children's mother deserted them years before, though she turns up in some episodes and connects with several storylines). First a steadfast maternal figure and provider, Fiona eventually has run-ins with the law. The father, Frank (William H. Macy), is a self-proclaimed patriarch but focuses more on his addictions to drugs, sex, and alcohol and his ability to cheat his way through life than on his offspring. The remaining five Gallagher children, Lip (Jeremy Allen White), Ian (Cameron Monaghan), Debbie (Emma Kinney), Carl (Ethan Cutkosky), and Liam (Brenden Sims), represent an eclectic, somewhat perverse, and a quite possibly unique set of characters. Filtered through the experiences of this group of characters, viewers understand that life is a struggle just to assemble the resources necessary for survival.

A larger scenario shapes the characters and situations of a television comedy, contextual elements filtered through the conventions of the genre. If the setting of a show is lower-middle-class America, then it follows logically that American capitalism is part of the framing scenario. The system of American capitalism is rooted in the practice of *laisse-faire*, or free, trade. Rather than centralized regulation, the access individuals have to property and wealth is the fruit of their ability to pull themselves up from the "bottom" (poverty) and build their lives. Within this system, some become winners while others become losers, forming a natural hierarchy. It follows according to this system, then, that those at the bottom have been placed there by their misconduct (Cohen and Antonio 60-62). The system focuses on the perceived merits of individual citizens as the basis for establishing their social standing. American capitalism celebrates those at the "top" of the hierarchy while simultaneously criminalizing those positioned at the "bottom."

A postmodern interpretation of *Shameless* will allow us to unmask many of the biases and implicit messages embedded in the media text. Postmodernism celebrates a form of art that transcends material boundaries and limits to provoke relationships between the material and immaterial (Blair, Jeppeson, and Pucci 264-271). Blair defined postmodernism as a "disruption of the 'normalized'" to "reveal the non-necessity of what appears to be necessary" (265). In other words, the scenario framing the situation comedy points viewers, in many ways, toward the metanarrative of American capitalism to dismantle the rigidity of the metanarrative structure. Viewers understand the fragility of a broken, lower-middle-class family because they understand the structure of American capitalism. Throughout the show, the Gallaghers are characterized as a family that has failed because of its collective inability to make the "right" choices. The lack of agency all of the characters exhibit within the series (at one time or another) is demonstrative of American capitalism; the characters who fail to engage a proper level of agency to pull themselves up by their "bootstraps" are doomed, inevitably, to poverty.

In sum, the scenario of *Shameless* acts as both a context through which the characters navigate in attempts to find a resolution and as a microcosmic structure through which viewers can understand the metanarrative of capitalism in America. To put it differently, *Shameless* offers us a sample of what it means to be a White, lower-middle-class citizen in the United States during the early part of the twenty-first century. It is through the actions of this trying group of characters that viewers explore the burdens they carry within the show, but the series also creates a space for viewers to develop a sense of the experience of real people different from themselves and, perhaps, an to locate opening for developing empathy. Therefore, the scenario in which the series *Shameless* has been constructed can function as a tool to critique and explore metanarratives that seem external to the show itself. It is for this reason, and based on this larger context, that I argue *Shameless* represents a sub-genre of comedy that simultaneously celebrates the characters on the series and the critiques the context in which they endure and, occasionally, thrive.

Scenario and Survival

The Gallaghers are in no denial about their socioeconomic status. Often, the children of the family collaborate to gather the money and supplies needed for survival. Even the youngest, Liam, is expected to participate in the collection of resources. Early in the series, viewers catch a glance at the Gallaghers's routine as Fiona delegates assignments to each child to make the month's quota for rent, food, utilities, and supplies. Many of the requests are unorthodox, unethical, and illegal, which indicates desperation to secure the goods and a level of comfort with breaking the rules to survive. Such requests extend even to the youngest child, which is seen when Fiona asks Ian to steal milk from a local delivery truck. In fact, a great many scenes and storylines of the show center on the different strategies the Gallaghers devise to get the goods and on their keen instincts for obtaining what they need for survival. When 15-year-old Debbie becomes pregnant, Fiona insists that the young mother-to-be either have an abortion or find her own means to support the baby. Desperate for motherhood, Debbie decides to keep the child. She struggles for weeks to find financial stability until she stumbles upon the lucrative business of stealing and re-selling luxury cribs. It is obvious that questions of legality do not interfere with Debbie's need to secure the cash she needs. Frank Gallagher is frequently absent, but when around, he often models questionable morality. When he discovers that coverage for a transplant has been denied, for example, Frank concocts a plan to break his leg to derive income through insurance fraud, and the scheme is successful.

Obviously, the broader context of *Shameless* is not only American capitalism but, more specifically, poverty. As I mentioned, a scene, in the Burkean sense of the term, encompasses those material and immaterial structures that characters encounter and sometimes navigate. If the Gallaghers were affluent, their need to perform critical acts would be significantly reduced. Furthermore, if the Gallaghers had even a slightly elevated socio-economic status, their choice to act outside of the law would stem from a level of agency (range of choices) vastly different from that of the lower-middle class; their decisions to steal, lie, and cheat might originate from a need for adventure as opposed to essential for survival. The scenario of poverty creates context and a physical space leading characters to make these particular choices to create a specific result. *Shameless*, in many ways, is a celebration of how these characters use their agency to survive. Rather than submit to the pressures of poverty and give up on their goals, the characters comprising the Gallagher family employ keen survival skills that allow them to thrive in spite of adversity (yes, there are ups and downs, but arguably they do thrive if viewers keep expectations modest). Viewers recognize that many of the acts committed are illegal, immoral, and unethical, but they seem to forgive transgressions, which is most likely due to the lowering of expectations corresponding to the scenario of poverty in which the characters are situated. In this way, the show becomes a celebration of the various ways the Gallaghers exploit those resources around them, and both agent (character) and scenario (context) move to the foreground of the televised dramatic situation comedy, or "dramedy."

Colorism and Survival

After *Shameless* first aired on Showtime in 2011, the story immediately distinguished itself from traditional domestic comedies. The half-hour format is not the only generic convention that is broken here. At the center of this dramedy or – as I prefer to term it – comedy of exploitation lies Frank Gallagher, the family patriarch, who busily abuses drugs while Fiona struggles to raise her five siblings in his stead. As viewers tune in and follow the family members through various battles with prison, rehabilitation centers, con artists, the Department of Child Services, and more, fans soon realize that this is no ordinary family. Throughout the show, anti-stereotypical characters are developed to represent the quirkiness of this Southside setting. After a few episodes, it becomes clear that a goal of this series is to shine a light on the untold stories of lower-class families, particularly those stories centered on a dysfunctional version of Whiteness. In the development of a new tradition of the family, however, the evolution of the second-youngest son, Carl, reveals a perspective of Blackness as a utilitarian experience. His selection and deflection of traits that define Blackness demonstrate a problematic system of Whiteness that exploits particular bodies as resources for survival.

Whiteness Studies is a field of research that focuses on how race and ethnicity shape and intersect with people, art, and institutions to influence societies. The concept of Whiteness is a rhetorical construct that can influence the class structure, race relations, and governance in heterogeneous communities. Several studies have explored the esteem of Whiteness in society. A series of studies conducted in the 1940s, for example, found that when offered a selection of dolls, children in primary school attributed higher intelligence, better behavior, and general likeability to White dolls over their non-White counterparts (Powell-Hopson 1-7). In other words, from an early age, a system of Whiteness can help us define which bodies we value and which we do not based on colorism, a system of valuing White bodies over non-Whites as a chronic symptom of Western colonization. Another study found that employers are more likely to contact employees whose names sound White over those who appear to be more ethnic (Rachlinski 1197-1204). This research demonstrates not only that the system of Whiteness values White skin tones over non-White but also that other characteristics are associated with skin tones and valued accordingly.

Kennedy argues that "White" is viewed as a neutral race category and, therefore, the normalization of Whiteness shapes how we view and understand non-White groups (359-402). Individuals and groups are often evaluated by their ability to assume and uphold the system. Blackness, for example, can be understood as a bastardized deviation from Whiteness. Quite often, Black bodies are characterized as hyper-masculine, hypersexual, and less intelligent than their non-Black counterparts. In the same doll study, students characterized Black dolls as possessing poor behavior and lower intelligence. Whiteness serves not only as a tool for accessing privilege but also as a standard for defining and characterizing the value of Black individuals.

During the sixth season of *Shameless*, Carl is charged for and ultimately convicted of drug possession with intent to sell after failing to smuggle a sizeable amount of cocaine from Illinois to Indiana. Until this point, Carl's sole purpose for selling drugs is capital gain. Unlike many other gang-affiliated members, Carl joins primarily to meet his survival needs; the desire to sell drugs comes at a time where he is experimenting with different capital ventures to make money. After his conviction, he begins to reinvent himself for the purpose of survival in prison. He braids his hair, wears oversized clothing, and sports a bandana gifted to him from fellow members of his gang. He costumes himself in Blackness as armor against the war ahead. Carl uses this appropriated version of Blackness to establish power within the Chicago community. While serving his one-year sentence in juvenile detention, he emerges as an unlikely leader within the Black community. Over time, viewers witness the rise of Carl's hyper-masculine demeanor and rich usage of Ebonics as a language. When he is later released, one might expect Carl to "return" to his "normal" self, a likely outcome of code-switching. Instead, Carl does the opposite – he maintains this sense of Blackness upon release to terrorize local small business owners and build upon his previous reputation. Quite often, his close family friend Vi (Shanola Hampton) criticizes his abuse of Blackness. Writers even pair him with a tall, 300-pound, Black partner, Nick (Victor Unuigbo), to define the form and purpose of Blackness. The two continue to use the fear and violence associated with gang members of color to patrol the streets as Southside Kings. Before long, Nick returns to the prison system for the brutal murder of an innocent, neighborhood child, which leaves Carl to define Blackness on his terms. Carl soon realizes that he is better off "going straight" and removing himself from the community he forced his way into earlier when it suited his purposes. He undoes his braids, changes his attire, and softens his harsh demeanor toward others, but he is not yet free. It is time to face his boss and stop dealing drugs for the older man's organization once and for all. After buying his freedom with a collection of clothes and a vehicle, Carl gives up the violent street culture and is finally redeemed. Blackness, once a utilitarian experience that provided security, has become a sin from which he finds redemption.

The use of Blackness as a journey demonstrates a great irony in this show's plot development: in an attempt to re-define "normal," the writers of *Shameless* exploit the Black experience as a resource for survival. For the writers of this show, it is convenient to reduce Blackness to a costume and to have characters wear it in moments of protection then dispose of it at will. It should be noted that there are numerous ways to engage the experience of Black individuals and to evoke themes of peace and leadership over violence or to present themes of communal survival over gang violence and that the characters of this show have been constructed to make a particular set of choices in the name of survival.

Discussion

This exploitation of Blackness as a resource is problematic to Black communities for several reasons. First, defining Blackness by and about Whiteness reinforces power systems that benefit those "neutral," privileged bodies. In an age when shows like *Black-ish* are redefining Blackness from "within" the community, narratives such *as Shameless* silence the efforts of marginalized individuals to build and establish autonomy. To reduce an entire community to a set of stereotypical markers is to dehumanize the members of that community. Next, this type of representation reinforces stereotypes of violence in ways that influence harmful activities off screen. One study found a connection between stereotypical markers of Blackness and criminal sentencing. The subjects were primed with images of "stereotypically Black" characteristics before being placed into a simulation with Black and White subjects. The study found that individuals who were characterized as being more "stereotypically Black" were more likely to be convicted and sentenced by both Black and White judges than White plaintiffs of similar crimes (Rachlinski et al. 1197-1204). The reality of television in a postmodern era is that those narratives created on screen spill over into the very narratives that are used to understand diversity "off-screen." Therefore, series like *Shameless* frame viewer expectations and preconceptions and have tangible effects on the perception and treatment of Black individuals off screen. Finally, narratives of a utilitarian Blackness perpetuate a myth that Black individuals choose certain stereotypical markers over others. These prejudices tie back to the notion of choice within American capitalism. The logic of the narrative follows that all individuals have an equal opportunity to make the right choices to thrive. Therefore, those who remain at the lower tiers of the socioeconomic hierarchy are there because of their choices; watching a White individual choose to access then discard violent stereotypes primes viewers to believe that negative stereotypes are, in fact, willed by Black individuals. Carl's ability to assume then discard Blackness as a resource for survival creates the illusion that choice is the best, most expedient, way to escape and that those who remain in that negative context *choose* to be there.

Conclusion

    Shameless explores the intersection of race and class within the context of an impoverished Southside Chicago neighborhood. This scenario provides the setting through which these characters can explore the realities of American capitalism and develop a means for survival. Burke would argue that it is a scene of poverty that fosters the continuous choice of the Gallaghers to commit crimes and act in otherwise immoral ways. The Gallaghers often take it one step past mere choice, however, and into the direct exploitation of the resources around them. The comedy of exploitation builds on gentle parables of the past with a broader range of permissible topics to explore and a harsher language, verbal and situational, for exploring them, but it places limits on critical understanding to keep these narratives from reaching a richer potential. This limitation extends to developing Carl assuming Blackness as a means of survival as a central narrative in the sixth season of the series. The agency and summative choices of Carl and the other members of the Gallagher family demonstrate the problematic use of exploitation in comedy today. To create transformative narratives and inject that consciousness into the world outside of the screen requires producers, showrunners, and writers who fully appreciate the ideological and practical implications of creative choices and then infuse popular texts with complex – even competing – critical perspectives that invite change.

ORANGE IS THE NEW BLACK:
REDEFINING GENDER ROLES AND OVERCOMING HOMOPHOBIA

Corey Washburn

6.1 Cast members of Orange is the New Black, "Can't Fix Crazy."

Orange is the New Black has quickly become Netflix's most-watched original series and has been nominated for several awards including the Primetime Emmy Award for Outstanding Guest Actor, the Golden Globe Award for Best Performance, and the TCA Award for Program of the Year (IMDb). The series, which is based on a memoir, revolves around Piper Chapman (Taylor Schilling), a woman living in New York City who has recently been sentenced to 15 months in Litchfield Penitentiary, a federal women's prison (Kerman). Piper has been convicted of transporting a suitcase full of drug money for her girlfriend, Alex Vause (Laura Prepon), who is an international drug smuggler. The offense occurred many years prior to the start of the series, and during the intervening years, Piper has moved on to a quieter lifestyle with her fiancé, family, and friends – a relative tranquility that the indictment interrupts and ultimately terminates. *Orange is the New Black* (2013-) represents characters that have not been frequently represented on television: members of the LGBTQ community. In this wildly popular series, viewers are introduced to explicit lesbian sex scenes, a transgender actress in a featured role, and the bisexuality of a main character – all of which are elements rarely seen in mainstream media, not to mention scarcely depicted all together on episodic television. This essay addresses the implications of gender roles and relationships as portrayed in *Orange is the New Black* and praises the series for innovatively integrating modern ideas and fluid identities into the sitcom while celebrating its potential for expanding the perspectives of closed-minded American viewers.

The original memoir by Piper Kerman, *Orange is the New Black: My Year in a Women's Prison*, articulates the reality of incarceration based on Kerman's personal experience and reveals many flaws in the prison system: the plight of women who are sexually abused by officials; the humiliation of strip searches, which are subject to happen at any time; and the otherwise tedious attempts to maintain relationships and connections with those living outside prison walls (Sullivan). The book also attempts, however, to bring light to the conditions of imprisonment, as the storylines include the beautiful friendships that can develop during incarceration, the joy of celebratory events such as birthdays, the culmination of unique friendships and mother-daughter bonds, and the gestation of new life, all of which help enlighten Kerman's prison experience. Contrary to the book, and significantly different from events in the Netflix series, Alex Vause is not housed in the same prison as Piper, and there is less lesbian interaction and relationship-turbulence in the autobiography than in the television series (Epstein). Why, then, were these elements of Piper's story exaggerated in the adaptation of the memoir? To make a point (or several), of course!

It is worth noting that prison is a defining element in situating these characters as the "other" to most of us. While I commend *Orange is the New Black* for including a more expansive representation of gender and sexuality than found in its source material or on most other series, I could have just as easily written about race and ethnicity, about social class, or about incarceration and its implications in separate chapters because of the depth and cultural significance of those ideas in this series. This complexity is part of the beauty of the series, and scholars are beginning to take note. April Kalogeropoulos Householder and Adrienne Trier-Bieniek in particular provide some meaningful interpretations of how feminism functions in *Orange is the New Black*. Specifically, their chapter "The Transgender Tipping Point" provides original perspectives regarding the discrimination Sophia (Laverne Cox) faces in Litchfield, overcoming transphobia, and exploring non-discriminatory friendships with other inmates.

Other scholars have explored feminism further as it pertains to broader audiences. In her article "Postfeminism Meets the Women in Prison Genre," Ann Schwan states that *Orange is the New Black* does not pretend to speak on behalf of *all* incarcerated women. Rather, "Piper's atypical viewpoint, conveyed through the conventions of comedy drama… [has] the potential to bring issues around women's imprisonment to a broader audience of viewers who are unlikely to consider them otherwise" (Schwan). Piper Chapman as a character allows us to see these flaws in the correctional system not only because of her "atypical viewpoint" but because of her skin color: White.

Unfortunately, we cannot know what we would be exposed to about prisons if a person of color were to represent the lead character in this series. Similarly (and unfortunately), the series likely would not have received the same praise or publicity if more of the lead actors were from minority groups. Piper is WASP-y and has enough class privilege to provide a link into the series for viewers who identify with her status, which positions her character to create a compelling portrayal of an "otherhood" that many viewers could not otherwise begin to imagine on a personal level. In this way, Piper Chapman serves as a catalyst for expanded thinking and a bridge for empathy into *all* of these areas – race, ethnicity, social class – and presents an opening for discussion of policy reform as the series tackles troubling issues such as the privatization of prisons. While all of these are valuable projects, sexuality and gender representations are at the forefront of the equation in my reading of the series and are therefore worthy of their own separate discussion in this chapter.

The choice by *Orange is the New Black* writer Jenji Kohan to tweak Kerman's memoir was certainly intentional, and the changes are monumental for the plotline of the series. Had Alex Vause not been in Piper's same correctional facility, we may not have been exposed to the same sort of questions about the fluidity of sexuality that we are currently exploring, and had Kohan followed Kerman's autobiographical plotline, the series would likely have a much harder time targeting themes related to gender and sexuality. Earlier, I mentioned that the series places several social issues to the table. Kerman's novel brings these same issues to the forefront, but in reinventing the series to include so many explicit examples of sexual behavior and sexuality, viewers experience a much more holistic representation of a group rarely pictured on television: the LGBTQ community.

Maria San Filippo, author of *The B Word: Bisexuality in Contemporary Film and Television*, notes in an essay published later about *Transparent* that the family sitcom is changing to incorporate more real, raw, drama-infused topics – reflecting the elements of the American family that are drastically changing (305-08). *Orange is the New Black* serves as a similar rendition of the "family" sitcom since these women are each other's family in a world that isolates them from their biological families. Through this representation of family, *Orange is the New Black* confronts real issues and acknowledges the harsh reality of life's devastating circumstances and people who continually let you down but also acknowledges that there are those who remain steadfast and loyal. In this context, not only is the LGBTQ community represented, but several identity groups within the LGBTQ community have distinct storylines in the series – including lesbian, transgender, and bisexual characters.

While lesbian relationships are represented on television, they are rarely associated with the protagonist of the show and even less frequently become popular subjects of critical discussion in mainstream media. Certainly, other series have not been nearly as popular as *Orange is the New Black*, which has been covered in mainstream publications and favored by some of Netflix's most avid viewers. Often, lesbian and gay relationships emerge in a subplot featured on a particular series, and if the TV show receives any sort of praise or popularity, it almost always comes from within: as in, the heterosexual actors who play heterosexual characters in the protagonists' relationships. *Orange is the New Black*, however, has proven that a show that focuses much more on lesbian relationships than straight relationships *can* become popular in commercial and critical terms. Although precise ratings are not available, evidence points to viewers becoming invested in the Netflix series from the very first episode, "I Wasn't Ready," and many viewers say they "binge watched" after becoming hooked on the first episode. Some media sources have written about it as the most popular of the original streaming series on the platform (Ahmed 2017). Of course, we must note that the popularity of this show is not rooted in its representation of lesbian sex, but its popularity demonstrates that this element of the series did not "turn off" viewers from the show.

Orange is the New Black presents characters as people first without defining them solely by their sexuality; as their backstories are revealed one by one, viewers connect with them over time in an emerging relationship. By using flashbacks to develop characters incrementally, Orange is the New Black presents multiple characters as *humans* rather than *prisoners* – reminding viewers that the characters are individual and that they have lives extending beyond prison doors. Furthermore, friendships among the women are typically presented before romantic relationships, and viewers see much more camaraderie depicted in episodes than romantic involvement. For example, Dayanara "Daya" Diaz (Dascha Polanco) has an incredibly complicated story, but her toxic relationship with her mother and interactions with her group of supportive friends – Gloria (Selenis Leyva), Maritza (Dianne Guerrero), and Flaca (Marisol Gonzalez) – are far more prevalent in the series than her relationship with correctional officer John Bennett (Matt McGorry) even though her pregnancy is a pivotal plot point in the show. Similarly, Suzanne "Crazy Eyes" Warren (Uzo Aduba) is not represented as an obsessive lesbian but, rather, is portrayed as a person suffering from mental illness that has nothing to do with her sexuality. Suzanne's experience, like Daya's, is focused more on the people within Litchfield Correctional who keep her alive and help her work past troubling personal issues. The same goes for Nicky Nichols (Natasha Lyonne) and Lorna Morello (Yael Stone), who both have complex backgrounds but end up in a romantic relationship. Lorna claims to have a boyfriend outside Litchfield and later in the series becomes engaged and then married to a different man, and these storylines supersede her relationship with Nicky. For Nicky, too, her past experiences and home life becomes far more prevalent in her storyline than the fact than the romantic relationship she has with Lorna.

In this multi-faceted context, the lesbian relationships presented in *Orange is the New Black* have a different level of authenticity than is found in more one-dimensional characters defined primarily by their sexuality. The fact that these characters and their relationships are presented in a larger context without either idealization or denigration presents an opportunity to increase awareness and combat homophobia through the series. It was not until the 1970s that LGBTQ communities were represented other than minor roles in television series and movies, and even then, gays and lesbians were isolated in a primarily heterosexual environment rather than being presented as members of a larger homosexual community (Fejes & Petrich). *Orange is the New Black*, because of the inevitable isolation of people behind prison walls, creates a larger homosexual space for characters and less opportunity for lesbians to be seen as "other" among many of their peers. To put this into context, Pride.com lists only nineteen lesbian and bisexual television shows or movies that are cast with predominantly female actors (Gonzalez). While there certainly are other roles filled by LGBTQ actors, actresses, or characters, they are sadly underrepresented, and their roles are written in ways to contrast with their straight counterparts, a dangerous representation that helps construct and reinforce what counts as "other."

In addition to the lesbian characters in the series, *Orange is the New Black* features Laverne Cox, who became the first openly transgender performer to be nominated for a Primetime Emmy Award. She was also the first transgender person to appear on the cover of *Time* magazine. Cox plays Sophia in *Orange is the New Black*, a transwoman sent to prison for credit card fraud. Sophia is best known to the other inmates as the prison hairdresser, and she frequently gives advice to her clients. Sophia's role is a crucial one, not solely because Laverne Cox is a transgender woman in real life but also because Sophia is incarcerated in a women's prison after having previously identified as male. Facing discrimination, potential lack of friendships, and an eternal struggle to "fit in," Sophia encapsulates a broad representation of what it means to be a transwoman. As one might imagine, the hardships associated with a trans-identity pose all sorts of controversy as to how imprisonment is managed and how other convicts may feel about Sophia being part of their cohort.

To put this into context, Sophia undergoes a harsh confrontation with fellow inmates during the third season of the series when they attack her simply for being trans, despite her previous acceptance at Litchfield. The inmates enter Sophia's salon uninvited and harass her about what's "between [her] legs" and later ask to see. Sophia is then assaulted, a hate crime that should have resulted in harsh punishment for the bigoted perpetrators. Instead, Sophia is sent to the Security Housing Unit (SHU) allegedly "for her own protection," and since the orders come from Management and Correction Corporation (MCC), Joe Caputo (Nick Sandow) can do nothing about it. Sophia remains in the SHU for several episodes, which include some short scenes of her in utter isolation. The series portrays Sophia's situation as the fault of the administration, which deems her worthy of the SHU because she is transgender. Meanwhile, *Orange is the New Black* displays other members of Litchfield as finding Sophia's position in the SHU ridiculous with some expressing frustration that Sophia is held in the SHU so long without just cause. All this considered, Sophia's storyline reveals several important points about bigotry, injustice, and sexual and racial discrimination within the judicial system.

Fortunately, later in the series, Sophia is released from the SHU and even spends her last few days in the SHU with Piper Chapman, which gives her a glimpse of hope and reconnects her with friendship and the camaraderie that is a recurring theme in the series. Sophia's confinement to the SHU for much of the latter part of the third and fourth seasons of *Orange is the New Black* is certainly problematic, but also provides a realistic representation of what it is often like to be queer in a post-binary understand of gender identity. Sophia, though multiple members of the Litchfield community are also queer, somehow still manages to be boxed as "other" because of her trans-identity. Though the series presents many problematic scenarios for Sophia, her isolation is realistic and even grim. Yet again, the series demonstrates the implications of defying neat categories and makes visible a character crossing culturally constructed boundaries visible and makes her sympathetic to viewers of all types. It would be nearly impossible to incorporate a story about a transwoman without mentioning some sort of discrimination, and *Orange is the New Black* does not attempt to present an idealized world where all conflict ends with understanding and social justice always prevails. Where the series does triumph, however, is allowing space for Sophia to speak out against bigotry and discrimination and to stand up for herself in trying circumstances. Additionally, through these uncomfortable-to-watch representations, the series does allow viewers to understand and appreciate queerness better. The show also reveals flaws not only in the correctional system but in the judgments and language of the broader society and makes a call to action for viewers to treat everyone, including "others," with kindness.

Some *Orange is the New Black* viewers may see Sophia as a disruption to a women's prison because her gender assigned at birth would usually place her in a men's facility of the federal correctional system. It is clear from the series that Sophia would not belong with a population of male prisoners. This positions her as a redemptive figure in the narrative and demonstrates progress in terms of America's growing understanding and definition of gender. Either way, a character as complex and realistic as Sophia performed by an actress as accomplished as Laverne Cox on a show as well-regarded as *Orange is the New Black* is a milestone for modern television and may prove to be revolutionary. Following her success on the Netflix series, Cox became the first transgender person to play a trans character in a recurring role on a broadcast network series when she was cast in the CBS show *Doubt*. Throughout *Orange is the New Black*, cast members such as Cox (Sophia) and Polanco (Daya) have made high-profile appearances in campaigns to support racial and sexual diversity and have consistently spoken out against discrimination. A cynical view of this form of real-world activism by actors may classify this as "little more than the commodification of resistance, making use of protests as sites for publicity" (Artt and Schwan). A progressive view, however, celebrates the ability of LGBTQ characters to thrive on a streaming series *and* to be accepted while publicly advocating about their beliefs. Why should the celebrations of diversity (LGBTQ and otherwise) be confined to the screen?

Finally, and surprisingly, one of the most monumental aspects of *Orange is the New Black* rarely referenced on the series, and seldom seen on television at all, is Piper's bisexuality. When viewers first meet Piper, she is engaged to Larry Bloom (Jason Biggs), who promises to remain committed to her throughout her sentence. Piper reconnects with her ex-girlfriend Alex Vause (Laura Prepon) in Litchfield prison, however, which reignites feelings that may have never gone away. Piper Chapman represents bisexuality in a conflicting way – formerly engaged to a male, rekindling with her previous girlfriend, and continuously battling with her identity as straight or gay or bi. Ironically, Piper reflects on her relationship with Alex Vause as "just a lesbian phase" early in the series. Throughout the series, however, Piper undergoes an internal identity crisis in a troubling way and appears to be trying to place herself into one box or the other without ever formally recognizing (or at least admitting publicly) that she is attracted to both men and women and that the world is rapidly moving toward a post-binary understanding of identity in multiple ways. The ability of *Orange is the New Black* to advance the conversation about bisexuality bridges a gap that has been ubiquitous on television for far too long.

Piper seems to be troubled by her attraction to both Larry and Alex. She experiences a conflicting mental image of a binary representation of sexuality, one that reflects a difference in how she visualizes her life in and out of prison. Oftentimes, it seems as though Piper feels that she would only be attracted to Larry outside of prison, and she would only be attracted to Alex inside prison. For example, there are several instances in the series when Piper talks to Larry on the prison phone, her connection to the world "outside," only to turn around and talk to Alex inside Litchfield after she hangs up. This shows that Piper may be experiencing feelings of both straight and lesbian attraction, or simply that she may be unsure of how her life (and sexuality) would play out if she were not in prison. *Orange is the New Black* challenges that notion of fluidity through the judgments of other characters who continually ask about her sexual preference, call her names, or start rumors about whether she is romantically interested in boys or girls. Rather than choosing to accept one or the other, Piper ignores their comments and continues with her life regardless of sometimes harsh judgments from others. As with Sophia, *Orange is the New Black* allows a space for Piper to stand up for herself and respond to harsh comments or acts of malice within Litchfield in a way that provides a larger message for viewers who might be inclined to make strong judgments or reduce gender and sexuality into binary constructions.

Often, representations of bisexuality are negative, confusing, or otherwise vague on television or in movies. This is especially true when talking about women, as Maria San Filippo discusses in *Rescue Me* (2011). "Despite female characters' strong personalities- and those of the actresses playing them, including Gina Gershon, Tatum O'Neal, Susan Sarandon, and Marisa Tomei – it is hard to ignore that nearly every woman on *Rescue Me* is represented as either sexually demanding and emotionally unstable, or, alternatively, as sexually and emotionally withholding" (San Filippo). She goes on to state that these women's quests for personal and sexual self-fulfillment frequently endanger their children's well-being or even their lives, and never – not even in the case of the female firefighters – are we invited to see the women as heroes, too (San Filippo 2013). This powerful observation about *Rescue Me* can also be applied in Piper's case, especially if one was to look at prison as a redemptive experience for Piper after her engagement to Larry.

By not labeling Piper's sexuality, *Orange is the New Black* creates a fluid representation of Piper's sexuality, and the sexuality of other characters, largely by saying that it really does not matter. In keeping its characters on a level playing field regardless of their crimes, their racial, ethnic, and religious affiliations, and their gender and sexual identities, *Orange is the New Black* makes some powerful statements about what matters and what doesn't in a communal setting. In one instance, Larry asks Piper's brother Cal (Michael Chernus), "What is she, exactly?" To which Cal replies, "I'm gonna go ahead and guess that one of the issues here is your need to say that a person is exactly anything." Through dialogue such as this, the series directly confronts its efforts to keep Piper's sexuality fluid, despite the continuous comments by her peers such as "Piper the straight girl," "former lesbian," or "dyke" – all of which are either said about Piper or spoken to her face in Litchfield. Of course, just as in Sophia's instance, it would be incredibly unrealistic to feature a lesbian protagonist without some sort of confrontation with biphobia. And, again, *Orange is the New Black* does not attempt to mask the realities that face marginalized groups of any kind. Furthermore, it is not unusual for bisexual (or queer) characters to have difficulty articulating their thoughts and feelings about their orientation. Thus, creating a character whose story incorporates all the hardships often associated with identifying as LGBTQ is important and useful in taking us one step closer to seeing series built around protagonists who may be entirely proud of their bisexuality or other fluid identities regardless of what those may be.

Questions about sexuality, gender, relationships, and depiction on television are important for several reasons. First, the representations are important for what is portrayed to future generations of America. Jen Braeden, a lesbian sitcom writer, states that she struggled through her queer identity crisis via television (Braeden and Dalton). Through television, Braeden was able to not only find herself but comfort herself inside stories that the real world could not brutally interrupt. Even if children are not the direct viewers of these revolutionary shows, their parents may be. If these representations sway parents to incorporate a more inclusive, fluid representation of gender and sexuality, this will be translated to children's minds and perspectives, into schools, and ultimately, into adulthood. Furthermore, gender non-conforming children may benefit from fluid parental perspectives and may then feel supported in their own journeys through adolescence and into adulthood. Though the LGBTQ community is becoming more widely recognized and accepted, we are not yet close to a universal embrace of this consistently marginalized group. Counteracting avoidance and misrepresentations of LGBTQ characters on television and in other mass media is one way to make progress for future societies to come.

Another reason is because of the way we interpret the realities of other people – especially those of marginalized groups. We cannot continue to be the America that translates "Black Lives Matter" to "All Lives Matter." Instead, we must begin to understand intersectionality and recognizes that each group's struggle is a different one even if some oppressive structures are similar. *Orange is the New Black* uses individual characters to celebrate various marginalized groups and highlights aspects of daily life that are harsh realities for many people: racist comments and abusive from correctional officers; verbal and physical assault because of gender identification; and assumptions about personal character and moral beliefs because of one's sexuality. Through portraying these situations, viewers see a new reality for individuals they may not otherwise consider, which starts the conversation or, at least, the thought process that can lead to understanding and change. Additionally, *Orange is the New Black* shows that diverse characters can be well-represented on television series without sacrificing popularity. After the first season of the series, the narrative focus shifts from Piper to a broader representation of people in the ensemble cast, and many of these characters enjoy significant storylines within the collective social space. This representation is a radical portrayal of some real aspects of American life that contrasts sharply with mainstream media's straight, white history, a history of shows that rarely discuss these issues in substantive ways. Furthermore, it is worth noting that this show has been wildly popular on Netflix; although the streaming service does not reveal precise numbers of viewers, it has noted that more people watch the series than another popular offering, *House of Cards* (Wallenstein).Why, then, can't *Orange is the New Black* be mainstreamed? Is America not ready for that? I like to think that *Orange is the New Black* remains on streaming sites because streaming sites are quickly becoming the new way of viewing shows and movies – but unfortunately, I am not convinced that's the case. Perhaps the relative silence for complex and sometimes fluid LGBTQ characters remains on mainstream networks because we do not quite know how to articulate these situations appropriately yet. Perhaps it is because many of us are scared to explore or even incapable of even trying to understand people perceived as different from us. Whatever it is, *Orange is the New Black* brings vivid voices into this quiet place in the media landscape, separates itself from judgment or fear, and confronts real American issues while hysterically (and sometimes tragically) critiquing the criminal justice system. *Orange is the New Black* is boldly reconstructing American ideas through its characters and plotline, which is absolutely worthy of applause.

UNBREAKABLE KIMMY SCHMIDT:
SURVIVORSHIP AND DEPICTIONS OF HEALING

Samantha Rippetoe

7.1 Tina Fey as Andrea Bayden and Ellie Kemper as Kimmy Schmidt in Unbreakable Kimmy Schmidt. "Kimmy Sees a Sunset!"

Statistics from 2016 indicate that one in five women will be sexually assaulted in their lifetime, and one in three have been victims of (some form of) physical violence by an intimate partner in their lifetime (NCADV). Sexual assault and intimate partner violence is a prevalent issue and, for many, lived experience; television series have tackled the issue in many different ways but, remarkably, almost never in a way that focuses on the survivor experience after the trauma. Kimmy Schmidt (Ellie Kemper) survived 15 years in a bunker after being kidnapped by a mad Reverend (Jon Hamm), time spent without windows and without any contact with the outside world but always with hope. And though this is a very extreme example of violence toward women, the fact that the story is being told in a way that is thoughtful, instead of provocative, gives many women the chance to see themselves or some portion of their experience represented in the television series they are watching. *Unbreakable Kimmy Schmidt* (2015-) addresses how one woman, Kimmy, tackles stigma, post-traumatic stress disorder (PTSD), coping, and healing as a process without focusing the narrative on the violent events that created the trauma.

During the first season, the series centers around Kimmy's efforts to adapt to living outside the bunker, but everything she knows about life is based off the experience and recollections of a 12-year-old girl because that's how old she was at the time of her kidnapping. Through hilarious, endearing, and adorable scenarios, Kimmy ends up finding her place in New York City, develops a family structure through friendships, and breaks away from being a "mole woman." Storylines in the second season delve more deeply into the heavy emotional baggage that comes from being kidnapped and held against your will for more than half of your life, including how that experience affects relationships with close friends, lovers, and strangers. This chapter analyzes depictions of survivorship in the series and Kimmy Schmidt's strategies to combat the gendered violence in her life. *Unbreakable Kimmy Schmidt* establishes themes that portray the experience of survivorship as livable and survivor focused, which constructs a narrative model that allows viewers to empathize with Kimmy's journey rather than to spectacularize it. In this chapter, I will analyze the depiction of the eponymous character's experiences, categorize coping strategies that Kimmy uses to deal with the violence in her life, and analyze her healing process and the reconciliation of her past to develop healthier, ongoing relationships with others and with herself.

Survivor Focused

Though the premise of the show is largely based on Kimmy Schmidt's past as a captive confined to a bunker with three other women – the media later labels them "mole women" due to the fact that the bunker where they were imprisoned was underground – the only depictions of this time period are short, 10-second scenes that show only brief moments from her captivity. These scenes are usually vignettes of her and the other imprisoned women doing different things that help them make the bunker livable, including pretending to drive a car, having staring contests, and reenacting movies for each other. Though these scenes are extremely funny, it's definitely humor that comes from a dark place. The focus of these scenes never depicts explicit violence enacted upon them by the Reverend, though there are often allusions to it. The storylines are usually structured around how these women survived as a group instead of focusing on the man who trapped them there, making this a story of survival and resilience rather than victimhood.

Though never explicitly said, it is implied that Kimmy and the other mole women have experienced sexual violence while in the bunker, perhaps also physical violence, and certainly psychological trauma. This is shown in the way that Kimmy reacts to certain actions made of people around her. In the first season when Charles (Andrew Ridings) covers her eyes from behind, she reacts by immediately pushing and kicking him away from her. When Dong (Ki Hong Lee) tries to kiss her during the second season, even though it is consensual, she can't help but react involuntarily by hitting him over the head with a telephone. Rape survivors are the largest group of people who have post-traumatic stress disorder (Foa and Rothbaum 1998, 35), and Kimmy receives this formal diagnosis in one storyline contained in the second season of the show.

During that season – in the episode "Kimmy Walks into a Bar!" – she meets Keith (Sam Page), an Army veteran who, after looking into her eyes, determines that she has seen some difficult things much as he did when he was fighting in the war. The show has an ability to let survivors of assault be able to stand at a distance while also being able to relate to Kimmy. Maybe most viewers did not escape from a cult and her particular harrowing experiences, but a lot of people are survivors of some type of trauma. Juxtaposing Kimmy with an army vet in such a way that the veteran recognizes their commonalities allows some pushback against the stigma associated with domestic and sexual assault and legitimizes the experiences of survivors by framing them as comparable to those of soldiers. In fact, Keith sees Kimmy as someone who understands his pain in a way many others do not. This connection between Kimmy and Keith allows viewers to conceptualize Kimmy's pain and life within the bunker without actually having to show it, which maintains the narrative of Kimmy having control over her own life by not spectacularizing while also letting the audience know that she has been through some terrible situations.

Though the show does portray how Kimmy's trauma lives with her outside of the bunker, the narrative framing of the series does not depict explicit violence committed by the Reverend during the flashback scenes. The spectacularization of violence that is notably present in other shows, specifically sexualized violence toward women (like in *Orange is the New Black*), is not the focus in depicting the lives of Kimmy and her cohort. This narrative emphasis says something powerful about the show in general: when violent acts are committed, it is not a totalizing experience, and those acts do not singularly define an individual. This framing allows the show to delve into Kimmy's survivor experience in complex ways that often include negotiating violence without making the violence her whole life story, an approach that is truer to lived experience.

Kimmy Schmidt is undeniably a survivor within the series. The plot situations and dialogue are able to create a full and complex person with sweetness and grit, a character deeply changed by the violence in her life but not defined by it. *Unbreakable Kimmy Schmidt* gives survivorship an authentic storyline by giving the eponymous character real problems to work through, problems with real symptoms (like PTSD), and problems that are relatable to other survivors. For a show that tackles such a dark and heavy subject, there is a surprising amount of nuance and contrasting emotional tones. Ultimately, the complexity serves verisimilitude because there is still joy in life for survivors who are working through the necessary steps to move on from trauma. For Kimmy, this ability to experience joy has a lot to do with the fact that she never views herself as solely a "mole-woman." This fullness of character centered by her ability never to go completely dark and heavy, allows for a narrative of recovery and moving forward instead of a story built around victimhood. The creative choice to focus elsewhere is not uncontested. Some critics find that excluding scenes of violence takes away from the realness of the story. I disagree because making Kimmy the narrative focus instead of capitalizing on the shock value of the violence in the bunker creates more opportunities for viewers to see themselves as the "unbreakable" Kimmy Schmidt. It is this focus on her journey *after* the trauma that paints her as a resilient model for recovery and moving forward, a virtual role model within the sitcom genre in unprecedented ways.

Strategies

Kimmy Schmidt has developed many strategies to help her deal with rough situations in the bunker, and she begins to use them in her life outside after her escape, too. During the first season, Kimmy explains to her employer Jaqueline White (Jane Krakowski) that she has a strategy from living where she used to live (Jaqueline doesn't know she is a mole woman at this point), which is that she would smile really big and jump up and down and yell, "I'm not here! I'm not here!" Other techniques she describes throughout the series include counting down from ten seconds (Kimmy explains that anyone can survive anything for ten seconds), imagining herself in a Disney Movie, and singing loudly. These strategies help Kimmy during flashback scenes when she is in the bunker by allowing her to not be overcome by hopelessness and despair about her complete lack of control over her own life. Instead, Kimmy continuously upholds the philosophy – inside and outside of the bunker – that by keeping her cool and using these strategies she does maintain some control (at the very least, control over her emotions in tough situations).

It becomes clear as the seasons progress that Kimmy's overly bubbly personality is not merely an expression of herself but a way to distract others and to move beyond the hardships in her life. As Lenika Cruz explains, "Kimmy's upbeat outlook isn't naïveté or stupidity so much as a survival technique she developed after being kidnapped in middle school by an old, white cult leader (Cruz)." Some of these strategies are used productively to help her calm down or to motivate her to get things done; at other times, these strategies are used to mask or push down emotions that were not useful in the bunker (such as anger or sadness). She tries to use these strategies to help make the world seem better, however, and really takes on the idea that the only thing she can control is how she reacts to things. The plot of the second season of the series delves into which ones of these strategies are helpful for living back in the world again and which ones, though necessary in the bunker, are limiting in the world outside. The process of discovery is very similar to that of women who have been in "ordinary" abusive relationships where women who are subject to violence like Kimmy (intimate partner violence and sexual assault) are likely to feel self-blame, shame, and negative social reactions (for Kimmy, being labeled a mole woman and seen as a spectacle by the media) that can lead to PTSD and depression (Kennedy Prock 6.). This series makes the choice to depict the journey back from kidnapping and captivity as one that includes both difficulty (such as living with PTSD and depression) and joy (like rediscovering yourself despite the past of violence) to reinforce the idea that people, particularly women, are more than the trauma they experience and have the agency to make choices that will improve their lives.

Healing

Kimmy makes the difficult decision during the second season to see a therapist. Television critic Alan Sepinwall describes this plot point as "where things started to get really interesting and complicated for the remainder of the [second] season" (Sepinwall 2016). The series does a great job capturing the fact that this can be a hard choice to make, even for people who have been in the most extreme and horrifying situations, because of the widely held belief that people should be self-reliant in dealing with the traumas in their lives. During the episode "Kimmy Goes on a Date!" in the first season of the series, Kimmy is having a dream that she is going on a date with Charles (Andrew Ridings), a tutor employed in the household where she works as a nanny. In her dream, the date starts off with the couple returning to her apartment in Disney-style princess and prince outfits, and Kimmy then informs Charles that she is going to change clothing. When Kimmy enters her bedroom, however, it becomes the bunker that she was trapped in for all of those years, and she is unable to get out. When Kimmy does wake up from what started as a dream and turned into a nightmare, she is choking her roommate and friend, Titus (Tituss Burgess), who is in bed screaming for her to get off. Titus then tells Kimmy that she needs to find someone to talk to about what it was like being in the bunker in order to stop the random moments of violence that are occurring without her awareness. As a survivor of something so stigmatized (a very extreme version of intimate partner violence and sexual assault), however, Kimmy does not want to disclose her situation to more people than she must. The stigma of being "mole-woman," to Kimmy, prevents her from living a fuller life and so she keeps this to herself. According to researchers, this is very common behavior among survivors of intimate partner violence and results in situations where stigmatization is associated with avoidance and lack of disclosure (Kennedy and Prock 6.). Kimmy portrays lack of disclosure by not telling her close friends, many of whom don't find out about her past until the end of the first season, and by finding creative ways to keeping her past secret (like introducing herself as Kimmy Smith).

Realizing that Titus is right, she tries to talk to Siri later in the episode about her problems resulting from previously being a mole woman (and Siri correctly responds, "That's messed up.") but ends up on a date with an older man who has dementia and, therefore, cannot remember anything she says to him. After talking with him for a long time, she realizes that it's not just saying things out loud that will help her feel better, but she needs someone who will understand and talk with her about her feelings. The narrative of Kimmy seeking help is one that is normal and doable. She doesn't automatically open up about her traumatic past but does have the ability to see that help could be beneficial. Kimmy's initial resistance and eventual realization that she needs help allow for a more complex and realistic narrative in which the main triumph for the character is not merely survival after intimate partner violence and sexual abuse but figuring out how to get help (and help yourself) after the abuse because it can't be done alone. For Kimmy, asking for help is a huge step, as it is for many survivors, and *Unbreakable Kimmy Schmidt* takes that process very seriously in the series by allowing Kimmy to make progress through small steps.

Kimmy doesn't find someone to talk her experiences through with until the second season. Kimmy meets Andrea Bayden (Tina Fey), an intoxicated woman who presumes Kimmy is an Uber driver in the episode "Kimmy Meets a Drunk Lady!" Eventually, it is revealed that Andrea is actually a therapist, a professional who is a totally different person when sober from the party girl Kimmy originally meets. Kimmy is convinced that she can help Andrea with her alcoholism and agrees to go to therapy. At first, Kimmy expects therapy to be able to cure all of her problems immediately, not understanding why she continues to have to go back to therapy, reveal secrets, and experience no obvious benefit. At one point, Kimmy even yells at Andrea about how she feels like she is being cheated and coerced into talking about things she finds traumatic for no purpose. Eventually, Kimmy starts to let herself see the effects of the bunker that she ignored as a survival strategy before, such as why she refuses to feel or express anger. A lot of her ability to eventually open up is because she has built up a community and has sought out professional help that does not produce miracles but, instead, provides a process to engage with and interrogate how the past is affecting the present.

This storyline allows the series to explore what it means to heal, suggesting that it is a process versus a switch that can be flipped from "traumatized" to "totally normal." Kimmy finds herself facing the frustration that many of us who make the leap to go to therapy face when she repeatedly asks the question, "Why am I not better already?" This perspective, along with a mix of the events and character traits that have shaped Kimmy, allows viewers to have a fuller picture of the possibilities presented when a survival story exceeds that initial set-up and allows the survivor character to become a whole person. By the end of the second season, Kimmy faces the fact that there is more to work through than she expected. This provides a storyline that is true to the complications that come with living through trauma and with going into therapy. This narrative encourages patience for those who are dealing with traumas by portraying the process of seeking help and healing as one that takes time and ongoing work. Kimmy is asked to monitor her anger and her feelings and to interrogate why she is feeling specific feelings at specific moments. All of these tactics are used in real life, and the emphasis on the longevity of healing allows other survivors to see themselves in Kimmy's journey. Healing takes time but is possible, and it is long past time for a television series to depict that process of survivorship and to help recalibrate the expectations of viewers who have experienced trauma or who are in relationships with others who have had that experience.

Conclusion

    Unbreakable Kimmy Schmidt depicts Kimmy just as that: unbreakable. The story of surviving patriarchal violence is one that is messy and complicated, one in which being vulnerable and being strong are not contradictory but, rather, come together to form a fuller and more nuanced story of survivorship. Undeniably, Kimmy Schmidt demonstrates the link between strength and vulnerability through her story and its focus on what she does in the face of violence, her tactics to combat it, and her choice to move beyond the mole woman years even when the journey becomes difficult. Sitcoms have tackled issues of sexual violence and victimhood in various ways but usually just, as Max Dosser notes in the first chapter of this volume, in "a very special episode" on the topic that is plopped into a series a series with little to no context. *Unbreakable Kimmy Schmidt* has opened up the space to explore what it means to be a survivor of violence over multiple seasons while striking a delicate balance that prioritizes humor without trivializing the situation. Characters like Kimmy in the mass media give women viewers a story they can relate to and admire while combating violence in their own lives, and the series provides a powerful message of hope through storylines representing life as still good and worth living after trauma.

Unbreakable Kimmy Schmidt is a show for the survivor, though others can also relate. Other series seem to want those that have not experienced violence to have a means to do so, but *Unbreakable* presents a story that lets survivors of violence see themselves as whole, productive, and able to move on, even with a dark past. This version of storytelling is not often one that is portrayed on television, and almost never as a main storyline in a series, but *Unbreakable Kimmy Schmidt* portrays healing as attainable and possible, and with so many people who have experienced some variation of the Kimmy's pain, it is nice that television has created a narrative celebrating resilience to inspire those viewers with humor and honesty.

MASTER OF NONE:
UNINTENTIONAL IMPLICIT MESSAGING AS
NEGATION OF ITS SOCIAL AGENDA

Serena Daya

8.1 Aziz Ansari as Dev Shah in Master of None, "Indians on TV"

We need to talk about *Master of None* – a show about Dev
(Aziz Ansari), an average, first generation Indian-American, guy
trying to make a living as an actor in New York. The first season
of the show won an Emmy for Outstanding Writing for a Comedy
with several writers lauding the series for its authentic
representation of Asian-Americans on screen (Lee; D'Addario).
Master of None (2015-) is structured around an intentional portrayal
of the upswings and hardships expected for any 30-year-old actor.
Episodes show Dev trying to make everything work – his career,
family relationships, friendships, and romantic relationships –
while also pursuing his passions and facing his fears. The name of

the show is intentional, as Dev is a true "master of none," and he demonstrates that lack of mastery throughout the first season. Additionally, the intentionality of self-reflexivity and understated portrayals of diverse characters on the show operates at the highest degree. In addition to that intentionality, the show is funny, charming, and authentic, which is no small bonus.

But (and isn't there always a "but"?), there are *unintentional* consequences of certain elements of the plot, important consequences that subvert much of the strong, critical perspective the series provides throughout the season. In the remainder of this chapter, I explore both the intentionality and unintentionality of the show in the following order. First, I briefly explore the ontology of the words *Master of None* and the assumptions one can make from the series based on the title. Then, I move to a critical-cultural critique of the show's intentional normalization of various tropes. Finally, I critique the unintended consequences of the plotlines and the lasting implications those consequences have on viewers.

Ontology of *Master of None*

In choosing the title for the series, creators Aziz Ansari and Alan Yang had to be very intentional with their choices. In their selection of *Master of None*, they were very intentional in constructing the message they wanted viewers to receive when making assumptions about the show based on the title. The title says to viewers that the characters in the show are not completely accomplished at any one thing. With its root in an English language idiom, master of none, is the tail end of the idiom. The full idiom reads: Jack of all trades, but master of none. The statement implies that a person can be good enough at most things to pass but is not an expert at any one thing. Generally, the idea that a person is a Jack of all trades is a compliment to that person. If someone is a

Jack of all trades, that person is considered broadly educated, well rounded, and useful. A person who is a Jack of all trades, but master of none, is still learning and growing with the hopes of becoming a master in more than one thing. Structuring the title of the series around the latter half of the phrase is a whimsical use of the well-known idiom. The creators did not want to come out and say, "Hey, this show is about a character who kind of knows some stuff about stuff." In titling their show *Master of None*, the creators succeeded in getting out the message to the audience that the characters in the show are growing in a clever and creative way. The main message viewers receive from the title is that the show is about a character (or characters) attempting to become Jacks of all trades.

The main character, Dev, is a Jack of all trades; he knows enough to get by but does not have a mastery of the material at hand to be considered an expert. He knows enough about acting to make a living, but is not trained in classical acting, nor is he good enough to get what his agent calls "*Friends* money" by booking a highly rated television show or film. As the show progresses, he is seen pursuing the "*Friends* money," thereby working to become a master in that field. At the beginning of the first season, Dev knows a little about being in a relationship with a woman, and as the season progresses, he develops a relationship and eventually has to make real life decisions about being with her. Dev pursues mastery of being in a romantic relationship. As the season progresses, the main focus is Dev's attempted mastery of social awareness. He knows a little about concepts such as stereotypes, feminism, and other ideologies – enough to get by without sounding like a complete misogynist, racist, pig – but not enough to make informed decisions about how those concepts intersect in his life. His attempts to master these intersections of identity are one narrative foundation of the series. *Master of None* has been lauded as successfully integrating multiple representations of identity into the show and also normalizing those depicted characters' relationships with the protagonist (D'Addario). Dev's desire to master his social sphere is evident in the social group he keeps and in the normalization of the diversity in his relationships.

Multiculturalism

With the show as a backdrop, the writers use Dev's life – as an actor in New York living his life in the best way he can day to day – as a method of cultural critique and a form of subversion. This method is called critical multiculturalism. Coined by Douglas Kellner, critical multiculturalism probes forms of domination and articulates normative perspectives from which to criticize (94). This framework allows the show to bring in a diverse swath of characters, from his parents to various friends, to demonstrate the (real) diversity in New York City.

Take Dev's primary friend group for example. His friends are Denise (Lena Waithe), a Black lesbian who wears masculine clothing; Arnold (Eric Wareheim), an average, but weird, White guy; Brian (Kelvin Yu), a handsome and successful Asian man; and, a slew of other friends who make brief appearances throughout the series. Each of these friend characters represents a diversity trope that was intentional in its casting but also carries with it a contrived veil, as if the creative team felt a need to tick off the diversity boxes. It is entirely possible that a group of four friends has the makeup of an Indian actor, a Taiwanese man, a Black lesbian, and a White dude. But, that grouping also opens up the show creators to criticism that they intentionally cast these actors in the roles to make sure all populations were represented in the show. The criticism does not come either from the roles these characters play or from the unlikelihood of their friendship with Dev. The criticism arises from the notion that the characters exist as they do from a pro forma sense of obligation so that the creators could claim broad representation on their show. I do not necessarily think having expansive representation on the show is a bad thing, given that any positive representation of marginalized characters is generally a good thing (that conversation is for a different time); I do think the writers and casting directors need to be careful in how these characters are portrayed on the show, however, and what their diversity adds to the collective purpose of the show.

Another very intentional aspect of the multiculturalism on the show is the portrayal in a few episodes of Dev's parents by the real-life parents of Aziz Ansari; having Ramesh (Shoukath Ansari) and Nisha (Fatima Ansari) included sheds light on Dev's upbringing as well as his traditional roots. His parents are portrayed as immigrants with thick accents. It is clear they are not trained actors, and they often speak with little inflection and real hesitancy. Dev's mother is shy, reserved, but very supportive. Dev's father is sage, funny, and brings a real joyful comedic presence. The use of real (untrained) people as actors on the show is refreshing, and carries with it a sense of authenticity and legitimacy. The idea behind it is that these really could be Dev's parents – because, after all, they are.

The whole point of the multicultural emphasis on the show is the notion that any person could be substituted in for these characters and it still could be someone's life. That is to say, this show could be about a Hispanic woman (or any other person) in Dev's position, and the show would not change very much. The actors are playing versions of real people and speak realistic lines of dialogue with stuttering and unnatural pauses. The situations introduced on the show depict something that could really happen, to anyone; it just so happens that an Indian man is the main character of the show. Where the show fails its critical multiculturalism test is its lack of self-reflexivity. Kellner asserts that a successful critical cultural study must relentlessly examine its own methods, positions, assumptions, and interactions, constantly putting them in question and revising and developing them (94). Given all the diversity on the show, it is a responsibility of the show to address how "not normal" that diversity is given the White standard present on most television. In a group of friends where the White person is the minority is not in line with the status quo of television shows, and that aspect needs to be addressed within the show. Self-reflexivity can be achieved by the show writers if they allow one of the characters to draw attention to the fact that in their group of diverse friends the White guy is the minority and how strange that is when they compare it to representation in society. It is possible to address those underpinnings in a funny way too.

The show also assumes a lot about what is "better" or closer to "reality" in terms of how diversity and representation are presented on a screen. The show posits that an average guy has a diverse group of friends (that is not necessarily true). A lot of people choose to keep friends who are from the same culture, people with whom they share identities, because it makes them feel safe. It posits that having diverse friends is better for you—that is also not necessarily true. If there are people who are different from you – people who are racists, bigots, or narrow minded – then that diversity is not necessarily better for anyone. While I do agree that diversity in thought is generally beneficial to anyone who is attempting to grow, this show can do better in its promotion and critique of diversity and its implications on screen. The foundation of the show rests on the notion that any person could be substituted for the main character and identify with the personal journey; and, that is just not possible unless the show draws attention to the intentionality in their casting choices and writing choices. *Master of None* as a critical multiculturalism critique falls flat because it does not actively question its own methods, instead drawing on assumptions that being different and diverse is better. Yet, that unilateral directionality limits its scope in audience, as well as what socio-cultural subjects it can tackle.

The show writers make choices to tackle socially relevant and salient topics then share those ideas through a cast of people who create diverse representations of real people. Such depictions must be made carefully and analyzed from all angles. The intention to represent a multiplicity of identities in the show can be praised, and the intention to tackle salient socio-cultural topics in terms of shaking up the audience's assumptions about each topic is also recognized. It is important for the show, however, to examine its own methodology in assessing each topic because in the process of attempting to make the show funny, the writers have created some unintended consequences.

Unintended Implicit Messaging

Throughout the season, Dev is shown to learn about relevant socio-cultural tropes, surrounded by his diverse group of friends. There is a theme present throughout the first season that has unintentional consequences for the message the show is trying to convey, however. When Dev learns about and implements a specific, socially progressive ideology into any part of his life, he experiences negative consequences personally. This pattern implicitly illustrates the idea that people will miss out on the possibility for success if they examine and implement a socially progressive ideology. In his essay "The Subject and Power," Michel Foucault states, "Domination may only be the transcription of a mechanism of power resulting from confrontation and its consequences" (785). With that, he asserts that by attempting to subvert a powerful ideology, the subject effectively acknowledges and propagates that very ideology. What I mean to suggest here is that the very intentional recognition of powerful dominant ideology within the narrative of the series and the lack of self-reflexivity among creators to alter its method of criticism has led to the creation of implicit messaging to viewers as a means to propagate the very ideologies the show is attempting to subvert. In trying to direct viewers to the more progressive and educated way of dealing with socio-cultural issues, the series serves only to propagate those issues as the dominant ideology. To support this claim, I will take a deeper look at two episodes of *Master of None*: "Indians on TV" and "Ladies and Gentlemen."

The episode "Indians on TV" brings up the issue of stereotypical portrayals of Indian people and, by extension, all Asians on television. Dev goes in for an audition and does not get the part because he refuses to perform a stereotypical Indian accent while he is reading for the part. After the audition, he has the following conversation with a friend, another Indian actor named Ravi (Ravi Patel), who auditioned for the same role. They are discussing a casting call that was just put out for a convenience store owner named Pradeep, a character who has "a funny Indian accent."

> Dev: Look, I get it. There's probably a Pradeep who owns a convenience store. But why can't there be a Pradeep, just once, who is an architect, or he designs mittens, or does one of the jobs Bradley Cooper's characters do in the movies?
>
> Ravi: Dude, I think about that too; I just can't wait for that. I gotta work. And look, in the meantime, I could do real good things with this Pradeep money.
>
> Dev: Well, at least they're getting Indian actors now to do those roles and not go on the "Short Circuit 2" route.

The exchange ends in a moment where Ravi answers the phone because his friend is lactating due to some protein powder he is taking. The very serious topic becomes a flippant series of remarks tossed off in the conversation rather than a lasting conversation, or even a stronger punctuation in the narrative, and bigger opportunity for reflection.

I understand that the show creators want to make the exchange funny. It is a comedy, of course, but the tricky part is finding the correct balance between the comedic interludes and the conversations Dev has about important themes. Viewers listen in on very real thoughts that I am certain Ansari has had about his roles in show business, and these insights must be handled with extreme care so that the subject matter does not get overshadowed by a comedic moment. In this episode, the serious conversation about authentic Indian representation on television is overshadowed by a weird moment about a random man who is lactating. With that conversation, the show acknowledges the dominant ideology, that Indians on television should be isolated to convenience store owners and taxi drivers with funny accents. The episode subverts that dominant ideology by having Dev and Ravi converse about that topic and critique that ideology. Then, unfortunately, the show undermines that ideology when Ravi ends the conversation to help his lactating friend, leaving Dev sitting in the coffee shop looking as if the conversation never happened.

Dev then auditions for a role in a show called "3 Buddies," a situation in which he and Ravi are both up for a part. The casting agents like both Dev and Ravi, but they cannot cast both because according to an email sent out, if there were two Indian guys on a television show together, it would become an Indian show. Dev makes the point that there are two White actors on a television show all the time, and it is called a show, not a White show. The casting directors want Dev to do a funny Indian accent as part of the role, and he refuses to do it. In the end, he does not get the part because he refuses to do the accent. Here again, the show acknowledges the dominant ideology by not allowing Ravi and Dev to perform together as well as requiring a stereotypical Indian accent to fit stereotypical expectations and get the part. The show attempts to subvert the dominant ideology when Dev refuses to the do the accent and by including dialogue revealing the ludicrous reasoning about what is considered an Indian show. Then the show propagates that dominant ideology when Dev does not get the part because he refuses to do the accent. The reality is that the episode raises good points about stereotypical representation of minorities on television, especially Indians and Asians, by bringing up the idea that Indian actors still need to work even if that means playing those stereotypical roles. When Dev questions the status quo and refuses to perform those stereotypical roles, however, he misses out on the opportunity for a breakthrough part that could make his career take off. What this situation says to viewers is not to challenge the status quo or they, too, will lose out, just like Dev.

Next, the episode "Ladies and Gentlemen" starts off by juxtaposing typical male and female experiences after leaving a bar. A female character is depicted being followed home by a belligerently drunk male who has earlier harassed her at the bar. Conversely, Dev and his male friend are shown facing their biggest trouble of the night: Dev stepping in dog feces. The stark contrast between the obstacles the two characters face after a night out launches the conversation in which Dev and his female friends talk openly about gender equality and feminism.

In the episode, there is a scene where Brad (Ian Kahn), the director of the commercial Dev is booked on, comes to the table and introduces himself to all the men at the table while ignoring Dev's new girlfriend Rachel (Noel Wells) and Denise.

Rachel:	So, there's a thing.
Dev:	What?
Rachel:	You didn't notice that? That guy only introduced himself to the men at the table. He went right past us like Denise and I were invisible.
Denise:	Yeah. He totally snubbed us.
Dev:	I don't know. I don't think that was intentional. You guys were sitting in the corner. He's probably just in rush.
Denise:	Yeah, well in his rush he managed to shake hands with two random dudes and Arnold. He didn't think we were important enough.
Dev:	I don't know. I feel like you might be reading a bit much into it.
Rachel:	We're telling you that this is something that definitely happens to women all the time. But, fine. Deny our perception of the world.

Arnold then makes a comment about how inconsiderate the Brad was because he shook his hand while it was wet. In an attempt to make the situation lighter, Arnold gets up in a rush to go wash his hands because the nasty director shook his hand with wet hands and then everyone else leaves the table. Dev is left confused as to why Rachel and Denise are upset with how he handled that interaction.

On their walk home, Dev and Rachel have another conversation about how he handled the situation with the director. Dev does not understand why Rachel jumps to the worst conclusion about a man while Dev chooses to believe Brad is not that bad. Dev asks if Rachel thinks he is some kind of sexist monster because he doesn't believe other men are all sexist monsters.

Rachel: I'm not saying that you're a sexist monster. I just think it's weird that your first instinct is to act like I'm crazy, defend Brad Honeycutt, instead of just believing me.

[Later in the conversation]

Rachel: What I'm saying they're a lot of little subtle things that happen to me, and all women, even in our little progressive world. And when somebody, especially my boyfriend, tells me I'm wrong without having any way of knowing my personal experience, it's insulting.

The scene ends with Rachel screaming, "I win" and running away, in a comedic moment. Yet again, what could have been a moment that had lasting impact on the audience is brushed off as a flippant conversation never to be discussed or thought of again. Technically, he loses the argument (and ultimately he will not end up with Rachel either). So the lessons she may have taught him about feminism and standing up for women can essentially be written off as moot. He can continue to exist as a privileged male without having learned anything. Yet again, the show addresses the dominant ideology, attempts to subvert it, and then continues to propagate that ideology by squashing the touching moment between Dev and Rachel and reducing what would be a monumental conversation in any relationship down to a fight during which the couple chase after each other in a cute, comedic way as if a big fight never even happened and differences can be glossed over rather than resolved.

Earlier, in the same episode, Dev and Denise see a guy jerking off in the subway, take a video for proof, and they make a citizen's arrest. They yell to the whole subway car that he is being lewd, and the passengers throughout the car applaud the two of them when he admits his wrongdoing. A little later, Dev is drunk at a bar where he is venting about the injustices women face in show business to Brad, the commercial director.

Dev: The whole spot, you know? It's these three guys who are having a barbeque and one of their wives come up with lemonade. Isn't the whole thing just antiquated?

Brad: [Agrees]

Dev: It's all around us man. I mean look at this Garden Depot spot. When they have the background actresses, they gotta get the hottest woman ever. We don't do that with the guys. It's never "Oh are these men handsome enough?" Uh, "Do they all have six packs?"

Brad: Never. They're all frumpy bags of pudding. No offense [to Dev].

The next day, Dev finds out that Brad took their conversation seriously, removed Dev from the speaking role he had in the commercial, and relegated him to the background in place of the women. Brad has replaced the three women as the main characters and put all the men in the background. Eventually, Dev is deemed not good looking enough for the background and is dropped from the commercial altogether. Once again, Dev's implementation of socially progressive thought into his life results in a career setback, which reinforces the idea with viewers that it's best not to mess with the status quo and risk facing a similar result.

You can argue that this episode is different in the sense that the women win in this episode, which is the point. The intention is to have Dev advocate for feminism, be a feminist himself, and want the women in his life to succeed and feel valued. There are two forms of advocacy in this episode, and both propagate the dominant ideology. Take the citizen's arrest example where Dev goes out of his way to stop the perpetrator of a sex crime on the subway. For his efforts, he is rewarded when the passengers on the train clap their approval of him. He gets to tell the story to his friends, and they also praise him. Later in the episode when Dev advocates for women to be more present in the commercial he is shooting, he is not praised publicly but instead loses his job. What that implicitly tells viewers is that there is a risk to standing up for what is right. If you stand up for what is right when you do not have to, you could have a lot to lose, especially when the stakes related to a particular action are personal.

Conclusion

Master of None gets a lot of things right. The title refers to a character making his way through life, trying to improve and to grow, and the show does depict that journey. The series intentionally brings in a diverse group of people to play the supporting characters and has an authentic feel about it as a show. The idea is that any person could take Dev's place and identify with various relationships and situations, and the show accomplishes the goal of "relatability" well. Following that achievement, the incorporation of critical multiculturalism into the show – where the writers use the main character's life to critique dominant social and cultural ideology – places the show is ahead of its time, even if the attempt is imperfect. In a lot of ways, the show is successful in talking about important tropes without sounding didactic. In their desire to make the show funny, however, the writers sometimes create unintended, contradictory messages in service of a joke or comedic timing. These implicit messages undercut the goal of subverting negative stereotypes. Why should viewers challenge dangerous and problematic stereotypes if they are just going to lose out in the long run? Why should viewers challenge stereotypes, rape culture, and gender inequality if they will not benefit from doing the right thing? These questions are what the second season of *Master of None* needs to reconcile in order for the strong social message to be communicated effectively.

THE SEXUAL LIBERATION OF THE ELDERLY IN
GRACE AND FRANKIE

Courtney Green

9.1 (Left to Right) Jane Fonda as Grace Hanson, Brooklyn Decker as Mallory Hanson, June Diane Raphael as Brianna Hanson, and Martin Sheen as Robert Hanson in Grace and Frankie, "The End"

Introduction

In the spring of 2015, Netflix debuted a new web television series that broke the mold in terms of how older generations were depicted on screen. *Grace and Frankie* is a comedy that centers around two couples in their mid-70s. Grace (Jane Fonda) is a type-A, retired cosmetic mogul while Frankie (Lily Tomlin) is a free-spirited, hippie art teacher. The two women's opposing personalities have resulted in their disdain for each other over the years. If Grace and Frankie had it their way, they would have avoided one another at all costs, but since their husbands work together, each has been forced to tolerate the other. Grace's husband, Robert (Martin Sheen), and Frankie's husband, Sol (Sam Waterston), are successful divorce lawyers in San Diego, and the irony about their occupations becomes apparent within the first few minutes of the series premiere.

Robert and Sol ask their wives to dinner over mysterious pretenses only to drop a bombshell: they are in love with each other and plan to marry. Naturally, chaos ensues, and to add insult to injury, Robert reveals that he and Sol have been carrying on an affair for the past 20 years. *Grace and Frankie* follows the women as they navigate the uncharted territory that accompanies being single in your mid-70s. This surprising shift in family dynamics forces Grace and Frankie to live together in the beach house that both couples once shared as they start their lives over. In addition, the two women are also forced to help their children cope with tumult that comes with having lives they have always known being uprooted and turned upside down. Grace has two daughters – Mallory (Brooklyn Decker), who is a stay-at-home mother, and Brianna (June Diane Raphael), who is the newly appointed CEO of Grace's cosmetic empire – and the sisters are equally shaken by the news that their father has come out as gay and plans to marry his longtime friend. In comparison to their mother's relatively stoic acceptance, Frankie's children – Coyote (Ethan Embry), a recovering addict and substitute teacher, and Nwabudike "Bud" (Baron Vaughn), following in the family tradition as a lawyer – are tested by their father Sol's relationship with Robert as they try to grapple with their new reality.

The sexual liberation of the elderly in *Grace and Frankie* works to denounce ageism by exploring the topic of seniors and sex and then rejecting the dominant stereotypes held about elderly people. This chapter will explore how *Grace and Frankie* celebrates the sexual liberation of its four main characters – Grace, Frankie, Robert, and Sol – by analyzing three specific episodes, "The End," "The Anchor," and "The Sex." In order to have the most accurate examination of the sitcom, it is essential that a theoretical framework be employed to serve as the background for why the characters in *Grace and Frankie* interact and communicate differently from typical sitcom characters because of their age. Lifespan communication allows us to understand how interactions evolve within a family as individuals increase in age and the harmful stereotypes that accompany aging (ageism). What makes this sitcom so intriguing is how it portrays situations that many audience members may feel don't have an impact on older individuals and forces viewers to consider – some of them for the first time – older people as sexual beings. The series *Grace and Frankie* has the ability to start meaningful and necessary conversations about topics that previously have been considered taboo for certain ages.

Lifespan Perspective

The basic reasoning for a lifespan perspective, or any lifespan approach, is to gain a better comprehension and description of human behavior throughout the years (Pecchioni et al. 4). The lifespan perspective works under the assumption that human development is ongoing for the duration of our life span (Pecchioni et al. 4). Lifespan communication refers to the description, explanation, and modification of the communication process across the life span (Pecchioni et al. 10). This is important to take into consideration when discussing *Grace and Frankie* because a major part of the sitcom deals with how each family member is struggling to figure out how to interact with one another after Robert and Sol's relationship is revealed. Throughout the series, it is evident that information is passed differently among the older adults (Grace, Frankie, Robert and Sol) than it is among their adult children. There is a sense of mutual protection because the parents want to shield their children from what they feel as unnecessary and hurtful aspects of the relationship between

Robert and Sol while the children want to modify how they talk about their fathers when in the presence of their mothers in order to protect their feelings.

Baltes's tenets of human development, when applied to human communication, also provide worthwhile insights on particular relational dynamics depicted on *Grace and Frankie*. Specifically, plasticity, historical embeddedness (person-environment interaction), and contextualism (person-environment interaction) can give us a basic understanding as to why certain characters in *Grace and Frankie* communicate in particular ways (613). Plasticity suggests that both age and life experience have an impact on our communication skills (Baltes 613). For instance, this may explain why Brianna, Bud, Mallory, and Coyote find it more difficult than their parents when it comes to expressing their feelings about their new familial situation. Historical embeddedness assumes that historical factors, such as changing societal views, attitudes, and beliefs influence development (Baltes 613). Therefore, historical embeddedness presumes that younger people, who have grown up in a time period where expression is encouraged, are more likely to disclose than people in older generations, who tend to be more private because they were not socialized to express concerns, opinions, and emotions. This tenet is particularly telling for communication between Robert and Sol and the fact that they waited decades to reveal their true sexuality. For younger generations watching *Grace and Frankie*, it might be difficult to understand why Robert and Sol would wait until they were nearing the last few decades of their lives to confess their true sexuality. But, the men grew up in a time when homosexuality was not discussed and were, therefore, forced to suppress their true feelings.

Finally, contextualism states that although the context of our life experiences varies, there is a connection between traumatic events and the age an individual was when the event occurred that influences communication preferences/skills (Baltes 613). Clearly, the traumatic event of Robert and Sol's affair and pending nuptials has a different impact on every character and is a crucial part of their identities and interactions moving forward. Throughout the series, Grace tries to withdraw as much as possible in an effort to avoid talking about her feelings and admitting her embarrassment. Frankie, on the other hand, is much more open to discussing the various emotions she has connected to the situation. Much like his former partner, Sol is extremely sensitive and feels every emotion that Frankie has, but his efforts to communicate with her are often shot down because she is not ready to face the situation directly. While Grace and Robert are very blunt with each other, Grace frequently expresses her disdain for Robert's lies; it seems as though she is only comfortable articulating her anger with the other characters. Robert is unapologetic in the way that he carries on in his relationship with Sol. He refuses to hide his happiness any longer, regardless of who finds his displays of affection to be insensitive. The main characters' behaviors also link to a specific facet of the life span literature that describes how individuals tend to communicate/act when they are at a later stage in their life span.

Later Life and Ageism

There are several characteristics of later life within the life span; those most relevant to cultivating a deeper understanding of *Grace and Frankie*, however, are social support, socioemotional selectivity theory, and stereotypes. Socioemotional selectivity theory (SST) works based on the assumption that as individuals grow older, their social networks become smaller and their priorities shift to focus on emotional wellbeing (Lockenhoff & Carstensen 1397). Social support becomes crucial in these later years because individuals do have less options for friendships, therefore those people who are present should offer the best forms of encouragement. We see SST as the framework that guides Robert and Sol's decision to leave their wives and move forward with their relationship. They realize that the majority of their lives is behind them, and in an effort to put their happiness first, the men remain true to themselves regardless of whom they hurt. Social support is evident in the dynamic between Grace and Frankie as they are the only people on the show who can relate to what the other is going through. Although we see resistance at times from each of them, ultimately Grace and Frankie realize that in order to hold their lives together, they must first be there to comfort each other.

Aging also comes with stereotypes known as ageism, or discriminating against individuals because of their age (Fisher & Canzona 391). These forms of discrimination can come in a variety of ways such as patronizing language (communicating with older adults as though they are children) and talking extremely slowly or loudly because of an assumption that older people can't hear. Ageism also occurs in the form of delegitimizing aspects of a person based on his or her age (Fisher & Canzona 391). As stated previously, this chapter focuses on the sexual liberation of the main characters in *Grace and Frankie* and the particular way in which the sitcom is able to achieve this representation of liberation. *Grace and Frankie* explores ageism as it pertains to sexuality with Robert, Sol, Frankie, and Grace, and it is only when these harmful stereotypes are examined that the show is able to successfully denounce them. This is, in part, because *Grace and Frankie* must first make the audience aware of that fact that what is occurring is ageism and that it is problematic. By taking the viewers on this journey of what older individuals go through in terms of being denied their right to explore and revel in their sexuality, the show is creating a dialogue about this often unintentional, but nonetheless damaging, aspect of our society. In order to become familiar with how the sitcom is able to condemn ageism, I have chosen three specific episodes that most clearly and effectively illustrate the sexual liberation of Robert, Sol, Grace and Frankie.

"The End"

The series premiere of *Grace and Frankie*, "The End," begins with the two women doing their best to exchange pleasantries as they wait for their husbands to join them for dinner. It's clear within the first few minutes of the sitcom that Grace and Frankie are complete opposites, and this hinders the women from getting along. Once their husbands arrive, an awkward air falls across the table, and it is evident that Robert is eager to share news with the women. He encourages Sol to say what is on both of their minds, but Sol – being more passive – is unable to express himself effectively. Therefore, Robert proceeds to rip off the band aid and tell Grace and Frankie that he and Sol are in love, have been having an affair for the past two decades, and plan to marry.

The revelation ignites a series of emotions in both Grace and Frankie as they try to grapple with the fact that their marriages have been based on a complete lie. Throughout the episode, we see not only the women but also their grown children struggling with their new reality. Bud, Coyote, Brianna, and Mallory all try to offer social support for their mothers during their time of crisis, but ultimately, Grace and Frankie must navigate their lives with only each other as their primary source of assistance. Perhaps what surprises both families most is not the fact that Robert and Sol are leaving Grace and Frankie but that they were leaving their wives for each other. Viewers can see this definitively during an interaction between the two couples in the opening scene.

Robert:	(To Grace) I'm leaving you. (To Frankie) And he's leaving you.
Sol:	(To Frankie) For this next chapter of our lives.
Grace:	(To Robert) You're leaving me?!
Robert:	Yes.
Grace:	Who is she?!
Robert:	Oh, it's not what you think; it's a "he."
Grace:	Excuse me?!
Robert:	And it's Sol. I'm in love with Sol. Sol and I are in love.
Frankie:	MY Sol?
Sol:	Her Sol.
Frankie:	You mean you're gay, and THIS is who you are gay with?
Sol:	This is who I'm in love with.

The wives are astonished, and more than a few viewers probably have the same response to the announcement.

In "The End," *Grace and Frankie*, much like instances on *Family Guy* (1999-) boost "queer resistance" despite the incorporation of "queer characters and queer themes" (Dhaenens & Van Bauwel 125). It is that supposed shock factor that causes Sol and Robert, although two of the main characters on the sitcom, to function initially as factors in the storyline that still "reiterates dominant ideologies that reinforce heteronormativity and oppress queerness" (Dhaenens & Van Bauwel 125). The same effect is seen in episodes of *Family Guy*, such as "Family Gay," where gay characters and themes are depicted but only in such exaggerated ways that they work to urge viewers that heterosexuality is the norm (Dhaenens & Van Bauwel 125). "The End" does not portray Sol and Robert as an exaggerated gay couple, but their sexuality – along with their age – does initially work to put more importance on the heterosexual life they are leaving behind than the authentic like they want to build. Throughout the majority of the episode, Sol and Robert's relationship is not taken seriously by anyone in their family because of their shock that these men are gay and the age at which they have chosen to come out. It is a painful pill to swallow when the men tell their wives they are leaving, but that pain is almost unbearable when Sol and Robert reveal that they plan to marry one another. Not a single family member thinks it is realistic that these men in their mid-70s should start a new life together, especially when that means their wives are forced to pick up the pieces. During much of the episode, viewers see the children console their grieving mothers while their fathers are pushed into the background. By the conclusion of the episode, the narrative focus does not shift over to Sol and Robert, however, *Grace and Frankie* does ultimately reject the idea that Sol and Robert's relationship is not valid due to their sexuality and age because, unlike in *Family Guy*, there is no "re-installment of the nuclear family" (Dhaenens & Van Bauwel 135). This can be considered progress toward equality, if careful or even halting at first. Sol and Robert's relationship is a fixture that remains in the series and eventually thrives in the narrative regardless of their age and sexuality.

"The Anchor"

"The Anchor" shows Frankie as she enters the television workplace with the naïve notion of establishing the "feminist ideal [of] sisterhood" right off the bat with her boss Brianna (Kutulas 126). Unlike *The Mary Tyler Moore Show* (1970-77), Frankie is not initially able to create a sisterly bond with Brianna because her age prevents Frankie from being taken seriously in the workplace (Kutulas 126). Brianna repeatedly shuts down every idea Frankie has due to her lack of understanding about the current business climate for the cosmetic industry. Additionally, Brianna goes against Frankie's wishes of having a completely eco-friendly product and patronizes Frankie when she confronts her about the new ingredients.

Brianna: You want your lube in every grocery store in America, right?

Frankie: And some of the more progressive car washes, yes.

Brianna: Okay well products like this can end up sitting on the shelf for a *year*, and they need a little help from spoiling. (Louder) Do you know how fast yams go bad?

Frankie: Yes. Six months.

Brianna: No.

Frankie: Then no.

Brianna: Do you want to explain to the Good Stuff people why your lube has a shelf life of three to five weeks, in a darkened room?

Frankie: MY lube is going to be in the Good Stuff stores?!

Brianna: That's the plan, also in the packet.

Frankie: I read the packet!

Brianna: You *just* admitted you didn't.

Frankie: Then why keep bringing it up?

Brianna: Oh, to shame you!

Not only does this interaction reinforce age stereotypes as Brianna blatantly admits to shaming Frankie for her lack of knowledge about her own product, but in this episode, viewers also see anti-feminist stereotypes of pitting women against each other. Neither Frankie nor Brianna is willing to back down throughout the episode, and eventually Frankie plots a way to force Brianna into hearing what she has to say about her product. The fact that Frankie refuses to be patronized by her younger boss illustrates the combativeness stance *Grace and Frankie* takes against ageism in the workplace. It is only when Brianna decides to take Frankie seriously that viewers see a semblance of hope that there may be a possibility of sisterhood between the two – not quite as strong as Mary Richards and her best friend Rhonda on *The Mary Tyler Moore Show* but civil nonetheless (Kutulas 126).

Although it may seem as though "The Anchor" does not relate to the sexual liberation of older generations, it does just that because the product Frankie is so passionate about is her self-made yam lubricant. It is important to Frankie that she has a level of autonomy in the mass production and distribution process of the lube because her product can be seen as an extension of her sexuality. As a woman in her mid-70s, Frankie is the unconventional choice to be the face of lubricant because she is not thought of as a sexual individual, period. She is overly protective of her lube and, in turn, her sexuality so that it gets portrayed in a way that she feels comfortable because too often the sexuality of older females is misrepresented or lacks representation at all. So, *Grace and Frankie* first takes viewers through Frankie's battles with ageism as they relate to sexuality and feminism within the workplace only to reveal that there is a light at the end of the tunnel for older individuals when they demonstrate persistence in the fight to be treated with respect regardless of their age.

"The Sex"

In "The Sex," viewers see Grace grapple with accepting the sexual limitations associated with the "motherhood mystique" but, in the end, refuses the stereotype (Feltmate & Brackett 543). The motherhood mystique is a script for "good mothering" that "treats a woman's sexual fulfillment as incompatible with the all-encompassing mother role" (Feltmate & Brackett 543). One character who faces the motherhood mystique quite often is Marge, the blue-haired matriarch from the long-running, animated comedy *The Simpsons* (1989-). Marge continuously struggles to excel within the confines of motherhood, trying to be a good mother to her children while remaining sexually active to please herself (Feltmate & Brackett 542). Although Grace's children are grown, her role as a mother never ends and, arguably, has expanded with the addition of grandchildren in her life. The restrictions on sexuality only increase as women age; as a result, there are little examples of the motherhood mystique in reference to the sexual fulfillment of grandmothers in sitcoms.

This taboo issue is initially reinforced in "The Sex" as Grace is hesitant about advancing her relationship with her new boyfriend, Guy (Craig T. Nelson). At her age, Grace is less concerned about how her sex life might interfere with her mothering or grandmothering than she is about her ability to perform (or even the mere thought of her ability to perform). Viewers are able to see this firsthand during a conversation between Grace and Frankie.

> Grace: (whispers) Can we stop talking about this now!
>
> Frankie: Why are you freaking out? Breakdown your emotions for me.
>
> Grace: Annoyance, irritation…
>
> Frankie: No that's what you're feeling about *me*, I'm talking about tonight. Are you nervous this will be the first time in 40 years that a straight man will see you naked?
>
> Grace: No, because the lights will be off, matter of fact I'm going to turn off all the lights in San Diego!
>
> Frankie: What about vaginal dryness, are you worried about that?
>
> Grace: I am now!

Grace is originally ashamed and embarrassed about her sexuality, but toward the conclusion of the episode, viewers see that Grace is able to embrace her sexuality regardless of her age – a development that happens in part because of the social support Frankie offers to her. Grace is able to feel more comfortable in her skin because she and Frankie are able to discuss these personal issues, which are relatable to both women. In comparison to Marge, Grace is able to maintain differing aspects of her life by rejecting the limiting script that the motherhood mystique so often places on women in sitcoms.

Conclusion

The representation of as many demographics as possible in entertainment is extremely important because media as the power to give viewers hope and comfort that they are not alone in the thoughts and experiences they face regularly. Creating more possibilities and reducing limitations in popular narratives opens up spaces outside of mass media, too, spaces for viewers to occupy in real life. Furthermore, it is not acceptable merely to depict certain individuals as they have always been portrayed in the past. Especially with new platforms such as Netflix that allow for less restriction in content and a lower audience threshold for a series to be considered successful, it is crucial for media to push the boundaries on what viewers are accustomed to viewing. Seldom do real-life experiences fall neatly into particular categories, nor do the individuals who go through these situations fit into a single box. *Grace and Frankie* is just one sitcom that has been able to highlight and then complicate different stereotypes. As more demographics refuse to be ignored or represented in stereotypical ways, it will become even more critical that shows such as *Grace and Frankie* appear to give a voice to those who need to be heard.

9.2 Lily Tomlin as Frankie Bergstein and June Diane Raphael as Brianna Hanson in Grace and Frankie, "The Anchor"

9.3 Jane Fonda as Grace Hanson in Grace and Frankie, "The Sex"

LOUIE'S RELATIONSHIPS:
A THOUGHT-PROVOKING TAKE ON WOMEN OR A
DEPICTION OF HIS MISUNDERSTANDING?

Kristina Kokkonos

10.1 Pamela Adlon as Pamela and Louis C.K. as Louie in Louie, "Bobby's House"

Louis C.K. is no stranger to exploring women in his comedic material, – as most male standups tend to do – and his dark sitcom, *Louie*, offers a fascinating take on his fictional character's romantic endeavors throughout five seasons. Traditional love interest archetypes are present throughout the show: the one-night stand, the romantic tragedy, the on-again-off-again skeleton of a relationship. Each time a female character is introduced, however, his encounters with them are hardly understandable and, in some cases, entirely bizarre. From a feminist perspective, this is potentially exciting and positive in the sense that female characters in a male-written, directed, and produced comedy are depicted as multifaceted and complex. But a comparison of these types of characters that Louie is interested in leads viewers to identify a commonality: they are all impossible to figure out. Juxtaposing four enigmatic, female characters in *Louie* raises the question of whether Louis C.K. is portraying women unilaterally as intricate beings or writing them all off as unmanageable, irrational stereotypes. I argue that the ridiculousness and purposeful incoherence of the series camouflages the perpetuation of these stereotypes, which is negative if not dangerous, in such a way that these stereotypes reinforce the already-skewed representation of women in media.

Louie C.K. began performing fairly unsuccessful stand-up comedy in Boston and New York City in the 1990s. After landing a string of staff writing positions – *Caroline's Comedy Hour, Late Night with Conan O'Brien, The Dana Carvey Show* and *The Chris Rock Show* – writing and directing the 2001 film *Pootie Tang,* and creating and starring in the single-season HBO show *Lucky Louie* (2006-2007), his break arguably came when he began releasing several full-length comedy specials. *Live at the Beacon Theater,* for example, was sold on the comedian's website for $5 and racked up over $1 million in sales within two weeks (Biography.com); then, in 2009, FX announced that it had picked up and would air *Louie* the following year. It is a show that C.K. has described as a combination of "short autobiographical comedy films, about his life as a single divorced father and comedian, with segments of him performing stand-up routines that would be thematically tied to the films" that was "unlike anything he's done before" (Itzkoff). *Louie* and its creator have been praised for pioneering "the filthy and emotionally fearless, auteur-driven and defiantly non-pandering genre of prestige comedy" (Marchese) and have become known for the show's tendency to push the boundaries of the sitcom genre. An article in *The Guardian* explains:

> … [Viewers don't] find that familiar sitcom structure. Of course it is filmed with a single camera and doesn't have a laugh track, but these days the same can be said for every 30-minute

show not on CBS. What is different about *Louie* is that viewers must recalibrate their expectations of what the show is every time they watch it. Unlike the *Big Bang Theory* (2007-), where you could watch an episode on mute while waiting for a plane at the airport and still understand what's happening, *Louie* offers no comforting (or numbing) familiarity.

The show's unique style, as well as both critical acclaim and a steady increase in viewership, has helped to launch the show's popular discussion within the media. Five seasons have landed the series several nominations and awards, including two Golden Globe nominations, 22 Emmy nominations with three wins, eight Television Critics Association Awards nominations with three wins, and four Writers Guild of America nominations with three wins (*IMDB*). The number of viewers who tuned into the premiere of season three almost doubled the number of viewers who watched the premiere of season one. Though the ratings were not as high as other popular comedies on FX, like *It's Always Sunny in Philadelphia* (2005-) or *Wilfred* (2011-2014), *Louie*'s five-year run did incredibly well for a comedy with such an unusual nature (Satran). An interesting and telling aspect regarding the viewership of the series is its divided audience; after the third season, an overwhelming 70 percent of viewers were male, which had increased from 64 percent in the previous season. Women "were much more likely than men to watch the premiere but not return for episode two; 34 percent of women between the ages of 18 and 49 who watched the premiere did not tune in again a week later" (Satran). What exactly, then, was it about that first episode that turned women off for the rest of the season?

I believe part of the answer may lie in the portrayal of female characters in that specific episode and, by extension, the series as a whole. Take, for example, Louie's girlfriend April (Gaby

Hoffman) in the premiere episode of the third season, "Something Is Wrong." She joins him for lunch at a diner, incessantly complaining about her job, and when Louie tells her that she should quit, her eyes narrow as she angrily says, "What kind of a thing is that to say to me? You should quit *your* job." Louie's large plate of ice cream then arrives, which she appears disgusted by, before insisting that they not have "the food talk." April notices that something is wrong with Louie and tries to get it out of him; though he vows that he is only tired, she refuses to accept that. She then runs through a list of things that could potentially be wrong with him before landing on the assumption that he wants to break up with her. Her shock turns into a denial of their relationship ("You can't break up with me because, well, I'm not anything to you. We're not anything…We've been nothing for six months"), and when he tries to tell her that he is not breaking up with her, she interprets it as wanting her to do it for him ("This is amazing. You're gonna make me break up with myself"). She finally says, "We shouldn't be together anymore," and leaves the restaurant. Louie is left alone at the table, first exhibiting bewilderment but eventually showing slight amusement as he continues to enjoy his ice cream.

April's character is depicted as a negative, blunt, and selfish girlfriend, one who rips into Louie for everything from his eating habits to his inability to communicate with her effectively – all of which makes her an unlikeable character at best and a stereotypical "nagging girlfriend" at worst. Listed as "one of the most common negative stereotypes there is" about women in relationships, one psychology professor points out that there is no male equivalent or counterpart; when men want something done, they are simply making "requests." Susan K. Whitbourne goes on:

> Women who ask their [partners] once, twice, or
> more to do what they want receive this pejorative

judgment regardless of whether the request is reasonable or not. McHugh and Harbaugh note that "there is little cultural acknowledgement of the nagging husband" (p. 391). It's not that men don't make requests of the women who are nearest and dearest to them, it's that the behavior is labeled differently depending on who is doing the requesting. By using the derogatory term "nag," a man trivializes the woman's request and at the same time puts her in her place. In other words, it's a double-edged power play. It saves him actually having to do anything in response to her request until he's good and ready, if at all. By resisting her efforts to mold him to her will, the man can look as if he's in control of when he agrees to the request. (Whitbourne)

Whitbourne also describes the "henpecked" male partner as the woman's victim, "desperately trying to escape her clutches, but she keeps harping away." We consistently see this dichotomy reinforced during the interactions between April and Louie. She first has a hostile, one-sided conversation with him, then is defensive and continues to harass him throughout the scene. Finally, she dumps him in the middle of a restaurant. At the end of the episode, April comes to his apartment to retrieve her laptop and briefly takes care of him when she learns that he has been in an accident. Upon leaving, Louie asks her to stay and implies that they should get back together. April, in another one-sided monologue, tells him that a future together would be potentially disastrous, and she asks him to just thank her for helping him and to say goodbye. He is silent again, which severely frustrates her and causes her to storm out. Both the initial shock April expresses when she first realizes that Louie wants to break up and her subsequent sympathy and inclination to help him after his accident do show that she is not a completely emotion-less character. Yet, her consistent anger and animosity toward Louie, which contributes to his victimized nature throughout their conversations, paints her as an extremely negative character and reinforces the "nagging girlfriend/wife" stereotype. Though the show presents April and many of Louie's other love interests as multi-dimensional, the confusing and often absurd behavior they exhibit perpetuates negative stereotypes about women that are already rampant on television. The following three examples of love interests in Louie aim to develop this idea further with a series of characters exhibiting the stereotypical features of women as irrational, indecisive, overly emotional, or just entirely crazy.

The very next episode of the third season introduces Laurie (Melissa Leo), a blind date Louie meets at a mutual friend's house. Though awkward and unpleasant in the beginning, the two decide to get a drink after dinner and end up getting along well. They are both visibly having fun, and everything about the date seems to be normal until they get into Laurie's car and she parks behind the bar to initiate an orally sexual encounter. Louie is surprised and reluctantly agrees, but when she asks for the favor to be returned, he refuses because he is not comfortable doing it ("That's very intimate, and I don't really know you."). Laurie launches into a tirade of disbelief punctuated with phrases like "How dare you?" and "You gotta be shitting me," and she eventually belittles and insults Louie (while also accusing him of being homosexual). She makes a bet that he will be returning the oral favor "in about three minutes" then, suddenly, she violently shoves his head against the car window, which smashes it, and forces herself upon him. The episode ends with Louie calling her crazy as Laurie's car drives out of the frame.

This simultaneous depiction of Laurie taking control of her sexual desires while ultimately frightening Louie with them allows the show to both empower and demonize her qualities as a female character. Lisa M. Cuklanz and Sujata Moorti's study of women in *Law & Order: Special Victim's Unit* highlights this dichotomy perfectly: they state that though the show's storylines "thematize and elaborate key elements of feminist understandings of sexual violence," they "condemn aspects of feminine behavior and character, including empathy and intuition" at the same time (303). They use part of Barbara Creed's idea of the "monstrous feminine" found often in horror films to assert that "often, women's sexuality is depicted as the underlying problem…revealing male fears of women's sexual power" (315). The fact that Laurie is so candid about oral sex (especially for a woman her age; Leo was 52 years old when the episode aired) initially adds a feminist tone to the scene; she knows exactly what she wants sexually, and she engages in straightforward behavior to acquire it. Her quick change in temperament after Louie refuses to "return the favor" demonizes that very tone – it says that women with specific sexual desires will go so far as to physically and sexually assault a man to get what they want.

Later in the same season, Louie becomes interested in Liz (Parker Posey), a whimsical bookstore employee, and he musters up the courage to ask on a date after several clumsy attempts at seeking advice about books for his daughters. He ends up giving a beautifully endearing monologue, noting that she "is young and beautiful and [he is] not either of those things." Noting that though her first instinct would be to say no, Louie maintains that he really just wants her to agree to get a drink with him without expectations. She agrees and is surprisingly charming, positive, and energetic. On the date, some things go incredibly well, like trying a variety of foods at a fresh seafood place, while others start out questionably but end up working out, like her asking Louie to try on a glittery dress at a vintage shop. And then, there are moments of shocking confusion about Liz's behavior. At the beginning of the date, she tries to order drinks at a bar, but the bartender refuses to serve her "after what happened last time." Liz storms off then lies about it to Louie. Afterward, she tries to convince Louie that her name is "Tape Recorder" and carries the pretense on for so long that he believes her. And later, Liz convinces Louie to climb numerous flights of stairs to get to a rooftop and when he stops halfway to catch his breath, she hits him and angrily screams at him to keep going. There are some really profound moments in these two episodes with Liz: for example, she is perched dangerously on the edge of the rooftop but reassures Louie that she's not nervous because she has no desire to jump, while stating that the reason the scenario makes Louie nervous is because a small part of him does. So, while some of what Liz says makes a lot of sense, the other unanswered mysteries tend to leave viewers feeling unsettled.

Liz embodies the "irrational woman" stereotype that is based on the notion that women are far more emotional than men. Though rational thought is widely believed to be superior to emotion, research has shown otherwise; "not only do people not make better decisions when they aren't emotionally engaged, without emotions, people cannot make decisions at all. Thus, emotions are fundamental to effective action" (Baddeley). Still, the idea that women are more emotional than men, and thus more irrational, is a universal one both within our society and those portrayed in media, and it can be viewed as a form of control in our patriarchal world. An article in *The Washington Post* clarifies this notion:

> 'Crazy' is such a convenient word for men, perpetuating our sense of superiority. Men are logical; women are emotional. Emotion is the

antithesis of logic. When women are *too* emotional, we say they are being irrational. Crazy. Wrong. Women hear it all the time from men. 'You're overreacting,' we tell them. 'Don't worry about it so much, you're over-thinking it.' 'Don't be so sensitive.' 'Don't be crazy.' It's a form of gaslighting — telling women that their feelings are just wrong, that they don't have the right to feel the way that they do. Minimizing somebody else's feelings is a way of controlling them. If they no longer trust their own feelings and instincts, they come to rely on someone else to tell them how they're *supposed* to feel. (O'Malley)

We saw this in the episode with Laurie, when her irrational behavior leads Louie to write her off as "crazy," and we see it again with Liz, whose partially-incoherent behavior leads the viewer to believe she is just another "irrational woman" in the series. A final, also damaging, generalization portrayed throughout the show is notion that women are indecisive, which is an idea most clearly inhabited by the character Pamela (Pamela Adlon).

Viewers are introduced to Pamela during the first season as the hilariously blunt, single mom whom Louie ends up chasing for the entirety of the series. Viewers constantly root for Louie, as they watch his hopeless but genuine attempts to tell her how he feels matched by how rarely she reciprocates in the way that he desires. Even when they are "dating," at least by certain standards, she refuses to give their relationship a label or to talk about any romantic feelings. Her actions often say the opposite; in one episode, she kisses Louie under the stars on their first real date, and in another, Louie allows her to put makeup on him then she initiates a sexual role reversal. The latter example, however, takes a classically confusing turn when Paula breaks up with Louie immediately after their sexual encounter. Her behavior is often portrayed as irrational like the women before and after her in the series, such as the time she gets rids of all the furniture in Louie's apartment without consulting him first or the way she continually expresses childish disgust at talking about her feelings. Louie never knows what Pamela wants, viewers never know what Pamela wants, and though she is brutally honest and seems to be an open book in some ways, she is often unpredictable and almost irritatingly contradictory.

The "indecisive woman" stereotype also borrows from the notion that women irrationally base their decisions on their emotions, which causes men to believe that they are incapable of making coherent decisions and are, therefore, impossible to figure out. This commonly-held opinion was actually debunked, however, in a book titled *How Women Decide*:

> …[the author] uses studies, statistics and interviews to highlight that women are, in fact, just as competent in making decisions as men. Furthermore, it's not that women are particularly indecisive — research shows men actually struggle with making decisions as often as women. But negative stereotypes about their decision-making abilities make women more anxious about making important ones. Couple this with the narrow tightrope women often walk: We're expected to be collaborative and share credit, yet when we do, we're penalized for being too dependent on others' opinions. (Tulshyan).

Pamela's general uncertainty when paired with Louie's visible frustration over it helps to uphold the negative stereotype despite the evidence presented above. The indecisive woman trope, in connection with the irrational/overly emotional woman trope, exists everywhere on television and has been proven to have serious consequences for women off the screen. Certain stereotypes of women – including one that views them as "incompetent decision-makers" who "are irrational and lack the capacity for moral agency and reproductive self-determination" – have real-life effects, including actually hindering the ability for them to gain sufficient healthcare (Cusack & Cook 56). If Pamela is a woman who seems never to know what she wants, fails to ever make definitive decisions, and acts irrationally, the writing of her character is reinforcing those negative qualities that undermine the reputation of women.

When looking at each of these women separately, it is easy to attribute their mysterious natures to the abstractness of the show's writing in general. The fact that his two, very white daughters have a mother played by a biracial actress (Susan Kelechi Watson), who is then played by a white actress (Brooke Bloom) during a flashback in the fourth season is one example of the show's sometimes inexplicable elements. The depiction of his mother as an unpleasant woman at the beginning of the first season and as a kind-natured one by its end is another. As Kaufmann quotes the creative force, "Every episode has its own goal. And if it messes up the goal of another episode... I just don't care." Louie is always the most rational and logical character – and as the star, the most obvious fit for the average viewer to relate to is Louie – but another reading is that events are filtered through Louie's perspective and that what he sees (and presents to viewers) is filtered through his own feelings at the time. Sometimes his mother is unpleasant (from his point of view) and sometimes she is kind-natured (also from his point of view), which leaves the viewer without a context separate from that filter. Of course, this complex way of thinking about the narrative may be out of reach for most viewers or may not suit their media consumption wants and needs.

When viewing Louie's romantic history and lining up these female characters' stories side by side, it is reasonable to say that the show perpetuates the idea that women are irrational, crazy, indecisive, and universally impossible to figure out, and whether this is a reflection of Louie's experience of them or some more "objective" accounting of events may matter little. Because the series doesn't follow any strict format and includes a lot of other strange and perplexing characters, one could also easily argue that the intent of the creative team is for viewers to interpret these woman as separate entities instead of using their depictions to fuel a generalization about women.

C.K. himself addressed a female viewer's complaints about his episode "And So Did the Fat Lady," which features Vanessa (Sarah Baker's) heartbreaking monologue about the realities of "dating in your early thirties as a fat girl":

> After I made the episode about the fat girl, I read a blog post by a young woman who was furious. She said, "I've been talking about this all these years and nobody gives a shit. The fact that this guy's being carried around on people's shoulders by some feminists makes me sick to my stomach." And I read it and I was like, "*You're totally right. I completely see that.* Would that make me go, *I better not touch that note again?* It's the opposite. It's exciting to be a flash point. It's a valid thing to have your feelings violated and hurt. Sorry, but it is." (Marchese).

In this quote, C.K. appears to use the logic of the rule-breaking nature of comedy and the ambiguity of *Louie* to welcome negative feedback from women while simultaneously excusing the show's repetition of negative stereotypes. Generalizations about women as perpetuated by the media are impossible to ignore, however, so

I argue that the show in fact enforces these negative stereotypes about women, regardless of what it might be aiming to do artistically or thematically. Though I do enjoy this series and appreciate the uniqueness of the characters that it presents, viewing these female characters as a narrative causes me, from my standpoint as a woman, to take a critical eye toward the otherwise progressive nature of *Louie*, a stance that ultimately undermines my viewing pleasure.

ODD MOM OUT: THE HUMAN STRUGGLE TO FIT IN

Katie Nelson

11.1 (Left to Right) Alice Callahan as Stephanie, Abby Elliot as Brooke Von Weber, Byrdie Bell as Simone Locker, and Ilana Becker as Danielle in Odd Mom Out, "Wheels Up"

It is odd for a network that prides itself on producing reality television shows to create a scripted series that satirizes the very shows that serve as its trademark. The half-hour sitcom *Odd Mom Out* does exactly this to the *Real Housewives* franchise, which is the linchpin of reality programming on Bravo TV. The world of extravagance and excessive drama seen in the various *Real Housewives* cities is mimicked by the scripted settings and situations of New York City's Upper East Side found in *Odd Mom Out* (2015-). The central force within the show is Jill (Jill Kargman), a real-life, Upper East Side socialite, who in the show declares herself to be the "odd mom out." A self-loving, fast-talking, unconventional mother, Jill is a cool mom. She has tattoos, likes rock music, and has underwear dance parties with her husband and kids. Despite the many things she is and does to distance herself from the other, stereotypical, Upper East Side moms, she is, in fact, no better than they are. It is basic human desire to strive for perfection (Burke 14). So, in her quest to be the best mom and the smartest woman she can be, Jill actually leans into the trap of luxuries that, ironically, she prides herself for avoiding.

Even though Jill believes she is outside of the bounds of what constitutes superficial life on the Upper East Side, she actually accommodates the behavior she claims to reject through the three major facets of her life in her roles as mother, wife, and friend. It is through the back and forth of her internal conflict that the series ratchets up the drama and uncovers the foibles of her human façade. Viewers may enjoy watching Jill's struggles and misfortunes, but what does this say about us as viewers? Often, Jill's desire to fit in with women around her and her lack of awareness of her own privilege reflect the experiences and perspectives of many viewers. I argue that Jill grapples with the pull between her authentic self and her aspirational self throughout the series, and the show ultimately fails because its trajectory favoring the aspirational self sucks viewers into the pole of Jill's experience oriented toward the vacuous and fantastic.

From the earliest days of radio sitcoms to the modern sitcoms on television and streaming services, American situation comedies have always questioned the complexity of social class. It is in sitcoms that characters "pursue, but never quite achieve, the American Dream… however, the characters tacitly accept the validity and possibility of achieving this dream, with little political or economic critique to the contrary" (Dalton and Linder 9). Typically, sitcoms are representative of the American middle class, or they are based on the narrative conceit that characters exist separate from the stratifications of social class. *Odd Mom Out* takes a U-turn from the norms of the sitcom and does not pretend that its characters transcend social class. The show does not buy into the myth of classlessness and, in fact, showcases some of America's "one percenters," those elites whose income places them in the very top group of households based on income. In doing this, the show is put into tension with the American dream, which suggests that all citizens have an equal opportunity for success and the accumulation of personal wealth through hard work. The show is of great importance as it speaks to the times and, more specifically, the 2016 presidential election.

In the first season of *Odd Mom Out*, Jill continuously grapples with her authentic self and her aspirational self in relation to her maternal role. Jill and her husband Andy (Andy Buckley) have three kids, and the pilot centers around two of them (see Screenshot 11.1). The episode "Wheels Up" focuses on Jill's pursuit of getting her twins into the best kindergarten possible. The decision about which private primary school applications she should submit for her children is highly dramatic and intersects with a storyline in which Jill and Andy learn that his younger brother Lex (Sean Kleier) has recently sold his company for $675 million. The sale dwarfs the news of Andy's promotion at work, and Jill says to her best friend Vanessa (K.K. Glick) that she "feels the pressure to get her twins into the right kindergarten." Jill wants her kids to have fun end enjoy being kids, but she also wants them to receive a great education like their more privileged cousins (see Screenshot 11.2). In order to make this dream happen, Jill must make like a chameleon and integrate herself into the private school crowd by schmoozing with other parents and impressing them with her kids' intelligence and accomplishments. It is during the pilot episode that viewers first witness Jill's desire to fit into the Upper East Side crowd, but she still maintains her authenticity and uniqueness overall at this early point in the series.

Once the twins' kindergarten applications are submitted, the waiting game commences to find out which school her children will be attending. The drama in these episodes centers on what is colloquially termed "first world problems" to contextualize the severity of these conflicts. It is during this process that Jill goes to school open houses in order to meet future teachers with the hope of making a wonderful first impression. As she learns from her sister-in-law Brooke (Abby Elliott), what really matters in the whole process is the impression the parents make not the evaluation of the children who will actually be attending the schools (see Screenshot 11.3). Therefore, when it is discovered in the second episode, "Vons Have More Fun," that the family Jill married into is related to a tiny line of royalty, the question comes up of whether or not a surname change to Von Weber instead of Weber would aid her children's school acceptance. It is throughout this process that the viewer sees an element of Jill's contradictory nature, a contradiction that fits within basic human nature. According to Cristina Biccheri, "motives such as fear of embarrassment or the desire to fit in are mainly defined by internal and unobservable cues," so even though Jill might not say so directly, she does not want there to be a wavering impression of her as someone who might not fit into the elite society she is now a part of (188). Even without a direct statement to this fact, viewers understand that the eponymous character cares what both her new Upper East Side in-laws and old friends think. She wants the best for her children, so she strongly considers becoming a Von, but she also hates and makes fun of the elitism associated the Von name and the process of adopting it.

Throughout the episode, Jill is pulled in two very different directions: to adopt the Von name and become more like the women she intermittently conspires against or not to adopt the Von name and remain true to her anti-conformist sentiments. At the end of the episode, it is revealed that Jill will not change her name despite the increasing pressure to do so from both her mother-in-law and sister-in-law. Jill's relationship with her children is ultimately a force supporting her authentic self because, despite the imposing influence of her in-laws and the society of "one-percenters" all around, Jill maintains a pure relationship with her kids. Yet, even in the most authentic and pure domestic arena, Jill still reveals hints of her aspirational self when she inserts herself into the private school crowd and considers the name change.

In her role as wife to Andy, Jill aspires to be the best spouse possible. She wants to please her man in the ways that she believes the other neighborhood wives accommodate their husbands. In this endeavor, however, Jill is again pulled in very different directions. During the first season of the series, viewers see Andy and Jill struggling with intimacy. They are either too tired to have sex or have children wanting them to be available at inopportune times. So, Jill grapples with whether she should spice things up or just be herself in the bedroom. The episode "Dying to Get In" features a situation in which Jill simultaneously withholds her desire to fit in with her peers and loathes them for their Upper East Side ways. Jill aspires to be a hot mom for her husband when, in reality, her husband married her because he fell in love with her authentic self. Like most people, Jill "underestimate[s] the power of social motives to influence behavior" (Bicchieri 188). Through societal influences, Jill is seduced into underestimating the effect of social cues in the lives of women residing in the Upper East Side. The constant conflict taking place within her about whether to be countercultural or to be the quintessential wife and mother in the Upper East Side fuels much of the dramatic tension on the series.

Another manifestation of this tension is related to the relationship Jill has with her husband's family. Of course, Andy wants Jill to be herself in front of the members of his family, but he also wants her to get along with them. A clear instance of this conflict occurs during the first season in the episode titled "Omakase." Jill and Andy, already struggling with intimacy, decide to get a babysitter and go out on a couples' date night with one of Jill's new friends. Of course, as influenced by the mores of the Upper East Side, Jill decides to take Andy out to dinner at a posh, new Japanese restaurant. The wonderful date night is destroyed, however, when they happen upon Andy's brother, his sister-in-law, and a group of their friends. Lex's wife Brooke sweetly asks the restaurant staff to pull up some chairs so they can all dine together. Little do Jill and Andy realize at first, they are in for a special, 11-course treat including culinary pleasures such as "one long noodle, a leaf with salt, and an empty egg shell" and other exotic, bizarre, and unfulfilling courses.

Throughout the evening, viewers witness Jill enduring the scenario of her worst nightmare. She rocks back and forth in her seat, picks at her food, and engages in all sorts of other child-like activities. It is clear that Jill has no interest in the whole ambiance of the evening. She desires no part of the elitist lifestyle exemplified by this situation, and yet she must deal with it in her role as wife. Andy desires for Jill to get along with his family, despite their antics, but he also wants Jill to maintain her distinctive (mildly non-conformist) personality. That night, however, Jill still must quite literally sit and play her part. Not all at once, of course, but little by little osmosis takes over until she becomes more infected by the dreams of this seemingly perfect life. The closer Jill becomes with her husband's family, the closer she is to becoming an aspirational, ladies-who-lunch-and-shop version of herself.

The same sort of contradiction between fancy pants and her own pants occurs with Jill and her friendships. Jill has a lifetime best friend, Vanessa, who always loves the juicy gossip Jill has to tell her, but who also plays an important role in keeping the "odd mom out" grounded by embracing the authentic elements of her personality and behavior. Throughout the first season of the series, Jill wavers between her desire for a friendship with her queen bee of a sister-in-law and her preference for sticking to the close friendship she has always maintained with Vanessa. A true test of friendship occurs in "Midwife Crisis" when Jill must assist Brooke in giving birth because her water breaks a week before her scheduled C-section. Not surprisingly, the last thing Brooke wants is to have it be known that she had a natural, vaginal birth. Brooke must maintain her image, and part of that image is to remain as unnatural and dreamlike as possible. This simultaneously horrific and heroic moment when Jill is literally elbow deep in childbirth and subsequent events that test Jill's friendship with Vanessa. Although Vanessa is a doctor, she does not have a child of her own child, which Jill perceives as lack of personal experience. When a hectic and challenging situation unfolds with the birth, Jill resorts to Google rather than her closest (and greatly qualified) friend for assistance.

During the dramatic process of childbirth, "the female only space is celebrated in prioritizing and panicking over the intimate sphere of pregnancy and motherhood" (Winch Ch.4). Vanessa is out of this loop, and therefore outside of the "private sphere" of female friendship, despite the fact that she grounds Jill and pulls her toward the authentic pole of her experience and herself. Because Vanessa is on the outside of this situation and figures as an afterthought in one of Jill's most terrifying experiences, Brooke and Jill bond in one of the most intimate ways two people can. The conflict of interest is clear, and while it is depicted through two women – Vanessa and Brooke – they represent two parts of Jill herself – authenticity and aspiration. Jill works to have both friendships, even though she seems to despise the women who make up her sister-in-law's social group. After the birth episode, viewers see Jill becoming closer to Brooke and more entrenched in her sister-in-law's social circle. It is as if the birthing experience bonds the two women at an emotional level and serves as the turning point in Jill's choice between the authentic and the aspirational. Ultimately, Jill turns toward the aspirational, and the show then fails as satire because there is no strong and enduring character left to hold society up to ridicule; satire requires characters and situations be situated in a critical context that calls out the negative elements of society to advocate for change (Teuth).

Although the sitcom formula of poking fun at the lifestyles of the rich and famous is not new, the way in which Bravo TV's *Odd Mom Out* presents an exaggerated take on the negative elements and implications of the lifestyle is quite fascinating. At the same time, there is a classical referent for what happens in this episodic narrative. In conventional narrative structures dating back to Aristotle, the protagonist faces both internal struggle and an antagonist. Unfortunately, the "odd mom out" opts in during this series and takes on characteristics of the opposing forces. As Jill struggles with a tug-of-war between hating the rich women shopping on Fifth Avenue and becoming a shopper herself, the complex nature of the authentic versus the aspirational narrative does not go unnoticed. There is great complexity within the many characters of *Odd Mom Out*, but as the show's protagonist, Jill's development and struggle to fit in is most intriguing. It is her constant struggle to juggle her role as mother, as wife, and as friend that defines the series. The whole show is built upon a grand loss of perspective, and it is this loss of perspective – surely something most viewers can identify with to some degree – that provides an opportunity to critique not just these characters and situations but the whole genre of reality television. What happens to the meaning of the story when the protagonist becomes one of the characters previously situated as the antagonist? The satirical lens, so promising at first as a critique of privilege and self-absorption, ultimately fails as viewers are sucked in with Jill uncritically into a superficial world of extravagance and self-absorption. There is not much room for critique let alone actual resistance in this scenario, especially when the main character fails to stay authentic and the competing values of aspiration are revealed to be hollow.

11.2 Jill Kargman as Jill Weber and K.K. Glick as Vanessa Wrigley in Odd Mom Out, "Wheels Up"

WHY THE LONG FACE? WHAT *BOJACK HORSEMAN* SAYS ABOUT DEPRESSION

Kevin Pabst

12.1 BoJack Horseman (Will Arnett, voice actor) in BoJack Horseman, "Later"

Raphael Bob-Waksberg was a young, amateur comedian trying to break into the television industry. He had just moved out to Los Angeles from New York, didn't know a soul, and was living in a small bedroom in the giant house of a "friend of a friend of a friend" in the Hollywood Hills. While sitting out on the deck one night looking out over all of Hollywood, Raphael was overcome with melancholy, feeling that despite being on top of the world, he had never been more lonely and isolated. And thus, the idea was born to create a show based around a character who had every success he could ever want yet still could not find a way to be happy.

A few years later, in August of 2014, Raphael's vision came to fruition on Netflix in the form of the platform's first original animated series, *BoJack Horseman*.

Though early episodes were met with mixed reviews, critics warmed up to the show as it progressed, and by the end of the first season, the show was a success with many critics applauding the second half of the season for developing a unique comedic voice and achieving a surprising emotional and dramatic depth. The second season, released in July 2015, received near-universal acclaim for continuing and strengthening what made the second half of the first season so memorable. Season three, released in July 2016, was similarly met with ubiquitous praise and regarded as both hilarious and heartbreaking: "It does what *BoJack Horseman* does best, allowing the most heartbreaking parts of life to leach into the genre that's meant to soothe them" (Nussbaum); "*BoJack Horseman* is the best of all of Netflix's original series, and one of the best shows on television" (Sepinwall). "Even in an era where the lines between comedy and drama are the blurriest that they've ever been, what *BoJack Horseman* is capable of doing is nothing short of masterful" (Chappel).

BoJack Horseman's popularity can be attributed to a number of factors, including its eclectic humor (a unique brand that blends sharp celebrity satire, goofy sight gags, and witty, fast-paced dialogue), its simplistic yet beautiful art direction, and its tremendously talented voice cast, which includes not only Will Arnett, Amy Sedaris, and Aaron Paul in the main ensemble, but featured guests such as Patton Oswalt, Angela Bassett, and Keith Olberman in recurring roles. Of all these worthy and highly praised components, however, the element of the show that has received the most acclaim and generated the most discussions is its portrayal of depression.

BoJack Horseman is a cartoon depicting a world where humanoid, anthropomorphic, talking animals coexist with humans; they work together and have relationships with one another (with no explanation as to how or why this world exists). The narrative follows the titular character BoJack Horseman (Will Arnett), a washed-up, has-been actor (predictably, a horse) who starred in the popular '90s sitcom *Horsin' Around*, a shallow and clichéd domestic sitcom in the vein of *Full House*, *Family Matters*, and *Step by Step*. BoJack desires to make a career comeback and be a well-loved star nationwide once more, but he struggles with alcoholism, substance abuse, and an intense self-loathing that makes human (and animal) connection difficult. Most of the show takes the form of a character study following a (horse) man who struggles to be happy but simply cannot find happiness. As one television critic observes, "it's one of the most unflinching, brutal, and empathetic looks at serious depression that pop culture has ever produced" (Thurm).

The series begins with BoJack hiring ghostwriter Diane Nguyen (Alison Brie) to author his memoir. BoJack's many insecurities are revealed as he starts to open up more and more in their sessions together. He eventually develops feelings for Diane, whom he sees as the only person who understands him. Unfortunately for BoJack, Diane is in a relationship with his career rival Mr. Peanutbutter (Paul F. Tompkins), a golden retriever who starred in the '90s sitcom *Mr. Peanutbutter's House*, a blatant rip off of BoJack's own *Horsin' Around*. Mr. Peanutbutter is nothing but warm and friendly (standard for a dog), but BoJack resents him deeply. At first it appears this resentment is not much more than rivalry, but it is eventually revealed that the hard feelings stem from Mr. Peanutbutter's ability to be happy and to like himself, something BoJack can't figure out.

BoJack takes out his resentment and self-loathing on those around him, be they random strangers on the street or close friends he's known for years. The one who receives the bulk of his abuse is his roommate Todd (Aaron Paul), a jobless, homeless slacker who crashed on BoJack's couch after a party years ago and never left. BoJack treats Todd like his personal human punching bag but won't kick Todd out because he's afraid of being alone and needs the closeness of simply having someone there. BoJack similarly directs much of his abuse and neglect toward his agent and on-again-off-again girlfriend Princess Carolyn (Amy Sedaris), a pink tabby cat. He relies on her to fix his problems and goes running back to her for a date or a little more whenever he needs emotional validation before turning around and ignoring her, neglecting her needs, and even verbally abusing her if he needs to vent. BoJack loathes himself and takes his self-hatred out on everyone else, but at the same time, he desperately longs to be loved or even just liked (and not in a necessarily romantic sense). Deep down, he feels unworthy of any sort of love, so whenever he gets close to receiving it, he sabotages himself.

In a cultural landscape riddled with problematic depictions of mental illness – from fear-mongering and victim-blaming in news coverage to stigmatization and stereotyping in film and television – when a piece of media portrays such issues with respect, honesty, and authenticity, it's a big deal. Furthermore, when this powerful narrative arrives in the surprising form of a cartoon show about a talking horse, it's a really big deal. *BoJack Horseman* offers the most sincere and honest look at depression currently on television (or online), an accomplishment made possible by a number of techniques, including its inversion of common stereotypes, its longstanding narrative emphasis on depression, and its advantageous use of the medium of animation.
Inverting Stereotypes

Part of why *BoJack Horseman* is so successful at depicting depression is because it recognizes the problematic and stereotypical depictions that came before it and intentionally inverts them. As many individuals' knowledge of mental illness is shaped by what they see in television and film, it can result in a misinformed viewer base when so many portrayals of mental illness are riddled with problematic. Instead of falling into oversimplified, pervasive tropes so common in other media forms, *BoJack Horseman* illustrates how those stereotypes are misinformed and flips them and, in the process, not only presents a more authentic examination of depression but one that is also corrective of problematic portrayals. *BoJack Horseman* turns two specific depictions on their heads: The Romantic Fix-All and The Tortured Genius.

Many modern portrayals of depression present the disease as easily solvable by romance. Be it due to the end of a romantic relationship or the loss of someone close or any number of reasons, the protagonist spends a period of time feeling "depressed." After moping for a while, a new love interest enters his or her life and suddenly all traces of depression vanish. The new boyfriend or girlfriend is a magic elixir, eradicating any grasp depression has held in any area of its victim's life, romantic or otherwise. Some perpetrators of these types of depictions include *Silver Linings Playbook* (2012), which promotes the patronizing narrative that professional treatment is nothing compared to the curative powers of a boyfriend or girlfriend, *500 Days of Summer* (2009), in which the protagonist's depressiveness hinges solely on the status of his relationship, and *A Single Man* (2009), which sees its central character overcome eight months of depression and suicidal fixations within a single day by meeting a new love interest. These types of depictions are guilty of not only presenting a relationship status as the sole determinant of depression but also equating depression to little more than loneliness. In reality, many factors play into the complex mental illness. These factors are pushed to the side or ignored entirely, however, in favor of a more simplistic representation. Moreover, the Romantic Fix-All stereotype suggests a simple and easy solution to depression, which problematizes understandings of how it really works.

In contrast, *BoJack Horseman* offers no easy solutions for depression. As BoJack's on-again off-again girlfriend and agent, Princess Carolyn (a pink tabby cat) tells him in the series premiere, "I don't know how you can expect anyone else to love you when you so clearly hate yourself." Later on, in an episode from the next season, she notes that whenever people (and animals) try to love BoJack, he shoves them away. This theme carries through much of *BoJack Horseman* as he repeatedly tries to establish meaningful romantic relationships. Not only do these attempts typically result in failure, but these relationships do not eliminate his depression even when BoJack is successful in his romantic life.

During the second season, BoJack meets Wanda, a network executive (and owl) who has just awoken from a 30-year coma. BoJack has been in the public eye for about as long and is known mostly for a minor television show (of which he is embarrassed) and for a number of scandals. Wanda has no knowledge of any of that, however, and meeting her represents an opportunity for BoJack to start fresh with someone who has no preconceptions about who he is or what he's like. This is a clean slate situation for the horse. They begin dating, and BoJack realizes he really enjoys spending time with Wanda and wants to continue seeing her, which is unlike his feelings about the vast majority of people he's dated over the years. They eventually move in together and fall in love, yet despite being in a satisfying, long-term relationship, BoJack cannot shake himself of the depression he persistently feels, a condition that causes him to lash out at those close to him. Eventually, friction arises in the relationship, BoJack and Wanda get into arguments, and everything erupts when BoJack lets his insecurities take over, telling Wanda, "You didn't know me. Then you fell in love with me. And now you know me." The clean slate is written upon, and the opportunity present by the fresh start is lost. BoJack feels he is only capable of being loved by someone if they do not know him because anyone who really knows what he is like could not possibly love him.

Another common trope is The Tortured Genius; in these stories, depression is the romanticized burden of an artistic mastermind or a brilliant savant. This depiction suggests the inner demons of mental illness serve as the source of creative success, which indicates an inherent link between creativity and mental illness, as if the torment is part of the gift (Klein). It may seem like a curse, but it is really a blessing because it leads to such artistic genius. This portrayal is grounded in the idea that "great art comes from great pain." While that certainly *can* be true, it is not always true. Great art can also come from great joy, great boredom, great luck, and many other sources. Moreover, great pain does not always produce great art. As Lloyd Sederer, medical director of the New York State Office of Mental Health, explains, "Sometimes you have the two combined. When you have geniuses who have such prominence, like Philip Seymour Hoffman or Robin Williams or John Nash, they make you think that this is more common than it is" (qtd. in Klein). The Tortured Genius trope romanticizes mental illness as a blessing and a curse; it is torment glamorized with a silver lining and the price to be paid for such creative brilliance. *The Aviator* (2004), *Amadeus* (1984), *A Beautiful Mind* (2001), *Frida* (2002), and many other films and television shows reinforce the illusion that this phenomenon is more common than it actually is.

BoJack Horseman also quickly does away with the idea of the tortured genius, making it immediately apparent that BoJack's former sitcom *Horsin Around* was no artistic masterpiece, that it did not come from a place of great pain, and that BoJack himself is no genius. He is an actor who made low-brow television entertainment in the '90s, a celebrity struggling with depression, but the success of the former is not due to the latter. For the most part, the pain BoJack feels does not result in insightful or enduring art.

There are a few exceptions to this generalization, as there are moments when traumatic experiences from BoJack's past do fuel his (uncharacteristically good) performance while filming a movie. More often than not, however, there is no connection between his mental illness and his work, and sometimes his depression even gets in the way of his art. During the second season, he moves to Arizona in the middle of filming a movie without a word to anyone, and his performance is scrapped entirely when replaced by a computer-generated, digital rendition. During the third season, it is revealed that he attempted to make an artsy, ground-breaking television series, what would be the masterpiece of his tortured genius, but his insecurities and self-loathing took over during development and drove the project to the ground. BoJack is tormented by his past and his inner demons, no doubt, but this does not lead to great art, does not make him an artistic genius, and does not bring him fame as a groundbreaking actor. It only leaves him feeling broken and alone. In this way, *BoJack Horseman* ditches the tortured genius trope in favor of a more honest and common embodiment of depression.

Whereas many other shows and movies feed into these and other stereotypes, often without realization of such a misstep, *BoJack Horseman* identifies commonplace problematic tropes, acknowledges them as such, and inverts them. In the process, the series actively fights stigma surrounding depression and depicts a more honest and authentic narrative, inviting a deeper understanding of what living with mental illness is truly like. It is important for these kinds of corrections to be made and for them to be made in the mediums that perpetuated irresponsible and stigmatized narratives in the first place. *BoJack Horseman* is a model for how other shows might be able to avoid and fix missteps in telling stories of mental illness.

Narrative Emphasis

BoJack Horseman is able to create such an authentic representation of depression because the show makes depression the focus of the series rather than the focus of an individual episode. Part of the reason why many shows produce such problematic depictions of depression is because they try to tell a full story in half an hour. Any single episode of television, no matter how well written and how thoughtful, is simply not enough time to develop a character's depression fully much less *solve it* as many shows try to do. Furthermore, this problem is not unique to the depiction of depression. The temptation within the sitcom genre to tackle a heady issue within a thirty-minute slot and call it a day gained prominence with the popularity of the "very special episode" in the 1980s. In these one-offs, the main character would come face to face with a serious problem never encountered before, usually drug or alcohol abuse, an eating disorder, or teenage sex. Prominent examples include: the *Family Matters* episode when the punch gets spiked, and Steve Urkel nearly dies; the episode of *Fresh Prince of Bel Air* when Will accidentally causes Carlton to overdose on speed; and the *Full House* episode when Stephanie is tempted to try cigarettes. Because these are sitcoms, however, the issues are resolved cleanly and easily by the end of the episode, the characters involved learn a serious lesson, and they will never make the same mistake again.

These "very special episodes" often attempted to teach a lesson and moralize about highly emotional or taboo topics. In this way, they frequently framed issues, such as bulimia or drug addiction, as morally wrong, avoidable, and fixable. These were represented as repugnant acts characters wrongfully chose rather than harmful afflictions with which they were burdened. The effects of the issue on the person living with it were not as important as condemning the issue itself and preaching the dangers of such issues to viewers. Disorders, illnesses, and addictions are stigmatized as bad choices rather than serious afflictions. Though the "very special episode" billing eventually fell out favor, this approach to dealing with serious issues persists. Many shows took up the format as their weekly formula, dealing with such issues in every episode. And many others continued the practice without the "very special" billing. As such, issues that take much longer than twenty-two minutes to depict adequately and engage with were boiled down to stigmatized stereotypes, depression being one of them. To depict depression, show its origins and effects, and provide a solution for it in thirty minutes is to over-simplify the mental illness (especially when there are no simple or easy solutions). Such a practice necessitates reducing depression to a stereotype.

BoJack Horseman does not treat depression as a one-and-done issue, however, but as an ongoing one. BoJack lives and struggles with his depression in every episode of the show. Making depression the focus of the entire series rather than a "very special episode" allows the series to be more honest in its depiction of what it is like to live with depression on a daily basis and permits more in-depth character development. For example, the series depicts BoJack's childhood through a number of flashbacks strung from episode to episode, highlighting his abusive and neglectful parents and the severe emotional damage of his upbringing. The show often focuses on his constant search for acknowledgement and validation from those around him, whether it is fishing for praise for his television show, demanding recognition of his star status, or begging to be told that he is a good person. And, as previously stated, the series is about a character that cannot find a way to be happy even when things are going well. The show takes its time across entire seasons to give BoJack the things he thinks he wants – money, fame, love – then to depict him failing to find happiness. All of these stories create a fuller and more thorough representation of BoJack Horseman, who he is and what his depression is like, which would have been much more difficult, if not impossible, to depict in a single episode.

By making depression the focus of the entire series, the show can illustrate from episode to episode the ups and downs of living with the condition, the impact it can have on relationships, and the extent of its influence on the life of someone living with it. Essentially, *BoJack Horseman* can and does provide a more thorough depiction that doesn't need to be over-simplified to fit within a mere twenty-two minutes; through its ability to be more detailed and extensive, it creates a more realistic narrative to tell the story of living with mental illness with surprising nuance and complexity. Within *BoJack Horseman*, depression does not operate as a single episode storyline but as the series-long narrative emphasis, which gives the show's writers the space to engage with mental illness in a far more comprehensive and authentic manner.

The Advantage of Animation

The medium of animation allows *BoJack Horseman* to create emotionally honest depictions of depression that would be much more difficult to accomplish in live-action television. The rather goofy and bizarre nature of the show (both in its premise and its humor) may seem at odds with its dramatic intentions, and it is counter-intuitive at first glance. As film and television critic Alan Sepinwall notes for *Hitfix*, however, "the sadness hits harder because it's coming right from a cartoon horse's mouth, while the preposterous comedy…feels even more welcome as a relief from the crippling despair" (Sepinwall). The humor and the drama actually help reinforce one another as each makes the other more potent. The very fact that the dramatic content is so unexpected because of the form of the show makes it resonate more loudly while the humor makes the dramatic material more palatable and digestible for audiences. Furthermore, *The A.V. Club*'s Vikram Murthi asserts that rather than inducing tonal whiplash, the shifts between the light-hearted and the heart-wrenching work well because the show doesn't treat comedy and drama like two different genres but, rather, like two sides of the same coin (Murthi).

Beyond the absurdist comedy made possible by animation, the mere fact that *BoJack Horseman* is a cartoon facilitates its engagement with depression. Mental illness is an abstract thing that can be difficult to visualize, and thus, a physically realist approach can have a hard time depicting the nuance of it with clarity. Some of the best portrayals of mental illness employ the fantastical and surreal, heightening reality to absurdist dimensions in order to show the far-reaching influence mental illnesses have on people living with them. For example, *The Independent*'s Stephen Kelly observes how Lars Von Trier's widely-lauded 2011 feature *Melancholia* is successful at portraying depression by setting the impending apocalypse as the backdrop for the depressed bride-to-be protagonist: "It does a great job of distinguishing depression from mere sadness, exploring the former's power to overwhelm just as any physical illness can when at its worst: neither her wedding day nor the coming apocalypse make any difference to Justine's condition" (Kelly). Another example is Jennifer Kent's 2014 horror feature *The Babadook*, which employs a dark, paranormal entity as a metaphorical stand-in for depression and guilt, a shadowy figure that is not representative of monsters and horror so much as "coming to terms with the dark side of human experience: mortality, fear, anger, grief" (Kidd).

These examples may be live-action, but they both utilize absurdist and surrealist storytelling techniques in order to enhance their depictions of depression. While this approach is certainly not impossible in live-action, it is far more easily achieved (technically and financially) in animation. And *BoJack Horseman* is not the only cartoon show that deals with depression and that does so effectively. *Adventure Time* features the depressed Ice King living at the top of an ice-cold mountain, isolated from most other living beings, and the series depicts his mental illness as originating from a magic crown that he cannot take off lest he die. *Rick and Morty* depicts a scientific genius – infinitely smarter than anyone else on earth so that he feels isolated from everyone – whose intergalactic and inter-dimensional adventures are often escapes from or embodiments of his isolation and depression.

Similarly, the absurdist world of *BoJack Horseman* is very much intentional and enhances its ability to evoke mental illness with an emotional honesty missing in other shows. For one thing, the lavish lifestyle BoJack lives and the insane and pricey things he spends his seemingly endless supply of money on are all easier to depict in animation than in live action. During the second season, BoJack buys a yacht, rides in it as it is towed across the country, and then sails across the sea chasing a cruise ship in order to rescue his best friend. While not impossible to depict in live action, such a plotline is certainly easier and cheaper to accomplish through animation. BoJack gets himself into similarly outlandish antics and goes to absurd extremes to try to escape, or at the very least to block out, his self-loathing and depression. He throws wild parties, often over multiple days, that result in substantial damage to his property; he goes on intense drug trips, which give him bizarre hallucinations and visions of the past, future, and alternate timelines of the present; yet, no matter what he does or what he buys for himself, he is unable to find happiness. That never-ending and seemingly futile search for what will make him happy is central to his character, and the true grasp depression holds on him is made clearer when his search goes to such extremes that are, more often than not, better suited for animation than live action.

What about the fact that the world of *BoJack Horseman* is inexplicably populated by talking animals? The approach certainly feels Brechtian, employing absurdism in order to focus viewers' attention on themes rather than characters or actions (Frimberger). Brecht often drew attention to the fact that his plays were representations of reality and not reality itself, constantly reminding the audience that what they were watching was constructed. Bob-Waksberg's show similarly disconnects itself from reality to such an extent that viewers are left wondering why. The very nature of the show invites viewers to engage with it critically and question what it is doing, which enables audiences to identify the themes and issues it presents more easily. As was Brecht's intention with his theater, audiences can approach *BoJack Horseman* with a critical perspective, become aware that the series serves as a commentary on living with depression, and understand messages better. Though these approaches to depicting depression and inviting viewers engagement through a critical lens are not impossible to accomplish in live-action narratives, they are well-suited for animation. As such, the very form the show takes enables *BoJack Horseman* not only to create a depiction of depression that resonates but also to encourage audiences to reflect on what messages the show attempts to communicate.

Conclusion

BoJack Horseman is an important show not only because it is good at what it does (and funny). It is important because the series gets right what so many other TV shows, movies, news channels, and other media sources get wrong. As M. B. Oliver asserts in her article in *The Journal of Communication*, audiences engage in not only hedonic, pleasure-seeking motivations but also eudaimonic, truth-seeking purposes while watching television and film; viewers are in the search for answers to questions addressing purpose and meaningfulness (984-985). While viewers are able to recognize events portrayed on screen as fictive, they are still susceptible to being influenced by general themes, characterizations, and treatments of issues on screen. Furthermore, because little education on mental illness is provided within public and private schools at all levels, many individuals get a majority of their information about mental illness from mass media, which can color their perspectives on what people with mental illnesses are like and how they behave, leading to fear, avoidance, and discrimination. (Tartakovsky; Wahl).

The stigmas perpetuated by these shows and films, and maintained by individuals who watch them, can have traumatic effects on individuals with mental illnesses as well. Fear of being stigmatized prevents many individuals from disclosing mental disorders they may be experiencing and, in many cases, prevents these individuals from seeking treatment. In fact, employees who have missed work for medical help would rather say they have committed a petty crime and spent time in jail than to disclose that they were admitted into a psychiatric hospital (Tartakovsky). Thus, the pervasive stereotypes upheld across various media sources not only lead to a misinformed public but have concrete, detrimental effects on people living with mental illnesses, which is no small portion of the overall population. It is reported that 43.6 million people age 18 or older, or 18.1 percent of all U.S. adults, live with some mental illness. Just over twenty percent of U.S. children aged 13 to 18 have been diagnosed at some point in their lives with a seriously debilitating mental disorder. Also, depression is one of the most widespread of illnesses, affecting an estimated 16.1 million adults (6.7%) and 3 million children (12.5%) (NIMH).

Clearly, current trends addressing depression and other mental illnesses on television and film are problematic for a multitude of reasons. Beyond perpetuating stigmas that create unfair representations of people struggling with afflictions, modern depictions of depression in television programs can have very concrete consequences for people actually living with the illness. Not only do these portrayals need to end, but as mass media serves as the primary educator about mental illnesses for most audiences, most current representations need to be replaced by accurate, honest, and empathetic depictions that will help mentally healthy viewers better understand these afflictions and help mentally ill viewers feel less alone and more comfortable disclosing their conditions to others. Luckily, a solid mold for this type of depiction already exists in the unlikely form of a gruff, binge-drinking, potty-mouthed, talking horse.

GIRLS AND POSTFEMINISM: THE FREE AND DETERMINED WOMAN

Leah J Haynes

13.1 (Left to right) Zosia Mamet as Shoshanna Shapiro, Jemima Kirke as Jessa Johansson, Lena Dunham as Hannah Horvath, and Allison Williams as Marnie Marie Michaels in Girls, "Beach House"

The HBO series *Girls* centers on Hannah Horvath (Lena Dunham) and three of her female friends – Marnie Michaels (Allison Williams), Jessa Johansson (Jemima Kirke), and Shoshanna Shapiro (Zosia Mamet) – as they navigate jobs, school, lovers, friendships, and existential crises as 20-somethings in New York City. Dunham is the creator, lead writer, and showrunner for *Girls*, co-producing it with Judd Apatow. *Girls* has been heralded for its dynamic female characters but also criticized for its narrow application of feminism by focusing on White, cisgender, heterosexual, able-bodied characters and ignoring the opportunity to feature characters representing identities facing oppression, those that would benefit from the deconstruction of patriarchal systems.

In addition the lack of intersectional identities in *Girls*, the show represents a move away from a feminist discourse that focuses on the social, economic, and political structures that oppress women and a move toward freedom and choices for individual woman, particularly women who are operating from positions of privilege. In these ways, the show is not unlike HBO's early 2000s hit show *Sex in the City* (1998-2004). Linder and Dalton (214) argue that *Sex in the City*'s focus on individual empowerment through consumerism (think of all the shopping), rather than the social, political, and economic advancement that liberal feminism seeks, limits its usefulness as a text to combat misogyny born of patriarchal systems. *Girls* suffers from this limitation as well. In fact, the pilot episode of *Girls* makes explicit reference to *Sex in the City* when Shoshanna claims that she moved to New York City explicitly because of her love for the show.

While *Girls* celebrates the complexity of the human experience as it relates to the individual woman, the benefits of dynamic female representation in the lead roles are undermined by the narrative detachment of the individual from the systems of society. Moving forward, I will use postfeminism as a lens by which to uncover the detrimental effect of *Girls* (and similar media texts and discursive threads) on efforts toward social justice and reform that art from a self-proclaimed feminist should support (either directly or contextually through critical readings). To describe something – a text, a culture, a moment – as being "postfeminist" is, in a way, exactly what it sounds like, a perspective that comes after, or exceeds, feminism. In other words, the term describes an expression of womanhood that assumes the social advances of Second Wave Feminism of the 1960s and 70s as a given, presenting women who have seemingly moved past a need to acknowledge systemic oppressions (Kissling). To describe a media text as postfeminist is usually to point out the ways in which a text takes gender equality for granted.

To describe postfeminism as an ideology, or as a lens of study, is more difficult, however. There is not definitive consensus on the term, particularly because it has been used in differing manifestations since the Women's Suffrage Movement to describe the state of women's social, political, and economic culture post-achieving certain feminist milestones (Orr Vered and Humphreys). Vered and Humphreys (2014) argue, however, that postfeminism is most indicative of the integration of neoliberal ideals – reduction of social welfare and individualism – into our assumption that the goals of Second Wave Feminism have been accomplished and incorporated into mainstream culture (157). It is important to note that postfeminism is not a replacement for feminist thought, nor especially of feminist critical analyses. It is reactionary and runs, at many times, counter to the goals of liberal feminism, discarding a focus on the "*structures* of patriarchy" for the belief that individuals are now capable and responsible for their own liberation (Orr Vered and Humphreys). To talk about postfeminist media is usually to do so through a critical feminist lens, and to mark the ways in which contemporary media representations of gender are harmful, even when they appear to be empowering.

Postfeminist media representations exhibit female empowerment as: (a) achieved through an individually-empowered mindset, (b) tied to the exclusively female body, and (c) experienced through sexual pleasure as both an act of consumption and as emotional and psychological gratification (Adriaens). *Girls* is certainly not the only example; postfeminist thought has manifested itself in popular culture steadily over the past decade. *Sex in the City*, as mentioned previously, is an example, but so too are *Ally McBeal*, *The Mindy Project*, and the *Bridget Jones's*

Diary films (Linder and Dalton) (Orr Vered and Humphreys) (Dejmanee).

As I have suggested, postfeminst media is problematic, though complicated; on one hand, it integrates qualities of a "liberated woman" into the daily experience of female characters —normalizing independence and female sexual desire, as well as making women's bodies a staple on screen. Dunham has a large measure of creative control over the show, and that is clear in the move away from figuring the female body from the exclusively male gaze. But, on the other hand, postfeminist media does not take any stance on, or responsibility for, the advancement of women's equity and often rely on tropes, assumptions, and language that feed into internalized misogyny. In the case of *Girls*, postfeminism also neglects intersectionality as a crucial theoretical and practical frame through which to view gender oppression, choosing instead to focus on how these women perform liberation while ignoring the real power of activism or the impact of structures like policy on the lived experiences of women.

In the following sections, I will highlight how these themes of postfeminist media – 1) focus on the individual, 2) an emphasis on feminine empowerment as experienced exclusively through the female body, and 3) sex as largely driven by consumerist notions of consumption and personal agency—appear in episodes of *Girls*, as well as how they relate to problematic narrative tropes that postfeminism perpetuates. These tropes limit what society considers possible, appropriate, or ideal for women, and, perhaps more importantly, downplay the legitimate societal, political, and economic barriers that women still face. Though Hannah, Marnie, Jessa, and Shoshanna may feel relatable to a White, 20-something audience as those viewers bumble through early adulthood, their attempts at liberation and authenticity make the characters of *Girls* convincing masquerades for pervasive misogyny.

Postfeminist Narrative Tropes

Postfeminist media is associated with a set of narrative tropes. In her 2009 book *What a Girl Wants? Fantasizing the Reclamation of Self in Postfeminism,* Diane Negra lays out the following plot points as salient among postfeminist movies and televsion: "return to hometown," "hyperdomesticity and self-care," "time crisis," and "working girls" (usually) with under-paying, less-than-ambitious jobs (Negra). Vered and Humphreys (2014) argue, building on Taylor (2012), that the "inevitable heterosexual coupling of the independent woman" should be added to that list. *Girls* contains episodes that utilize each of these narrative tropes. Exploring them individually, it becomes obvious that they are each built upon longstanding, gendered stereotypes that undermine Dunham's feminist goals for the show.

During the first season episode "The Return," Hannah returns to her hometown in Michigan for her parents' 30th anniversary. By leaving the city and engaging in a one-night stand with a classmate from high school, she questions her decision to leave home in the first place. Her ambition to exit the more rural, domestic space of her hometown and pursue the professional, ambitious plan of living in New York City and attempting a career in writing begins to seem like a mistake in light of the comfort of her parents' home and the normalcy of the town's residents. Hannah ultimately decides to return to the city, but it is only a late-night phone call from Adam (Adam Driver) that solidifies that choice.

Self-care and an emphasis on one's personal home space also appear throughout the series. Much of the plot of the first season is centered on the two-bedroom apartment that Hannah shares with various characters, and as the series progresses, that apartment becomes a safe space for Hannah as she faces failures in the public world. After being unceremoniously dumped by her boyfriend Charlie (Christopher Abbott) during the second season, Marnie finds renewed agency in a new apartment, diet, and workout regime. Finding renewal in the private, domestic life – even when accomplished without a man providing the finances for it – underscores the location of women's happiness in domesticity rather than in their public, professional lives.

In a related fashion, all of the women face significant professional failures and hold underwhelming jobs throughout the series. Hannah begins the series as an unpaid intern, loses two book deals, and quits all of the significant opportunities for a successful career – a lucrative job in advertising at GQ, an MFA program in creative writing at Iowa, and a job as an English teacher – before they can genuinely manifest in professional fulfillment for her. Marnie is fired from the art gallery where she works and spends time working as a personal assistant for a less-qualified woman while pursuing a career as a folk singer. Jessa works as a babysitter and a store clerk in a baby's clothing store. Upon graduating from college, Shoshanna fails at interview after interview. Most interest and disappointing, in terms of the depiction of 20-something career struggles, is that every failure seems to come down to a personal character flaw possessed by each of these women. Hannah is a narcissist. Marnie is uptight. Jessa is flaky and a junkie. Shoshanna is annoying and naïve. Every woman in *Girls* seems fundamentally incapable of thriving in the professional world. Is anyone successful professionally in this show? Yes, in fact, Ray (Alex Karpovsky), Shoshanna's 30-something ex-boyfriend and male friend of others in the group.

In addition to underwhelming careers, hyperdomescitiy, and a return to the hometown, Negra points to time crises as a narrative trope of postfeminist media. Hannah faces several time crises, particularly concerning writing deadlines, and the final episode the second season, "Together," centers on Hannah's difficulty finishing her book while staring at a 24-hour deadline. Hannah's inability to manage time could be interpreted as simply a character trait; Marnie, for instance, is almost always on time. Because Hannah is the focal character of the show, however, I believe that her poor time-management skills merit consideration. Alone, they may have be written off as a quirky aspect of Hannah's personality, but in conjunction with the other tropes that undermine these women's aptitude for things outside the home, Hannah's procrastination and inability to deal with the pressure that come with her book deadline (a tendency that is later mirrored, though less dramatically so, in her inability to spend her time writing for graduate school) speak to an overall theme of professionally incapable women.

Perhaps the most salient, and arguably the most anti-feminist, narrative trope of *Girls* is the "inevitable heterosexual coupling" that Vered and Humphreys discuss (158). I also conceptualize this pattern as a white-knight trope wherein the woman in *Girls* consistently experience crises or traumas that they themselves are the root causes of and that are ultimately remedied by the men in the series. At the end of the second season, Hannah – who for much of this season asserts her independence from her pining ex-boyfriend – breaks down from the pressure of her life and is rescued from herself by Adam. Seemingly inevitable, Adam's return is just what Hannah needs to be productive again. This is also evident during the third season when Hannah thrives under Adam's nurturing care. Even after her relationship with Adam concludes in the fourth season, Hannah finds herself rescued by her new boyfriend (and fellow teacher), Fran (Jake Lacy), who is just the normal, well-adjusted man she needs. In fact, as the epilogue to the fourth season indicates, it is in choosing Fran that Hannah successfully moves on from her toxic relationship with Adam.

Hannah is not the only woman "saved" by a man on *Girls*. Jessa, in the episode "Female Author" from the fourth season, pleads with Adam for his continued friendship after getting herself into yet another disciplinary situation—this time trouble with the police for public urination. She says to him, reluctant yet dejected, "I really need you to be my friend right now." Jessa's female friendships are not sufficient, especially with Hannah gone to Iowa for graduate school, and much like Hannah during the second season finale, she needs to lean on Adam for support. This is a continuing pattern throughout the first five seasons of the series with all four of the primary characters being saved from themselves by a boyfriend at one or multiple points along the narrative. It is the classic, white-knight trope. These women, though they flirt with independence, are represented as being in desperate need of a man to complete them and to fulfill the happiness they seek.

More important than their function as markers of postfeminism, these tropes highlight the continuing need for an organized and collective feminist movement. Even a show that depicts women who transcend the classic gender constraints of traditional sitcom – like motherhood and monogamy – depends on and subtly reinforces more misogynist stereotypes than may be obvious at first glance. The so-called feminism of *Girls* is undermined when women are represented holding unfulfilling jobs and in need of a man to put them back together after trying to "have it all" (Orr Vered and Humphreys). Continued feminist critique is clearly necessary; as Vered and Humphreys argue, the existing post-feminism seems impossible in light of the pervasiveness of these misogynist tropes (158).

The Free Woman

The postfeminist woman is also marked by her expression of what it means to be liberated, particularly that liberation is individually achieved and obtained through a celebration of the feminine through the female body and by a consumerist, personally gratifying sex life. Postfeminism situates female empowerment as individualistic rather than as social, political, and economic (Gill). The show's plot is driven by the personal and professional lives (and the intersections of those) of the four main women characters. Each episode's problems are idiosyncratic to Hannah (primarily) and her friends. Aside from the representative importance of complex female characters, the experiences of these women aren't generalizable, nor do they *push* for the social, professional, and civic equity of genders. A postfeminist woman is a free and self-determined one, or so she thinks. This runs counter to the traditionally feminist argument of the "personal-as-political." In her article "Postfeminist Media Culture: Elements of a Sensibility," Rosalind Gill argues that postfeminism has "reprivatized" issues that feminism once politicized while idolizing the concepts of personal choice and self-determination. She uses the example of postmodern women embracing Brazilian waxes and breast augmentations to "use beauty" as a means of self-empowerment and negating the systems that put pressure on women to subscribe to those beauty standards (Gill). *Girls* also prioritizes the personal, though mainly through Hannah's writing profession.

Hannah's writing is largely experiential and diary-like, and her character has the tendency to frame each issue presented in the show (sexuality, sexual health, career choices, etc.) as personal to her. In fact, her self-centered nature is presented as her primary character flaw in the show, and her self-absorption can be read as a critique of the postfeminist personalization and privatization of issues that face women. The show lacks this outright critique of the hyper-personal, however. *Girls* prioritizes Hannah's limited perspective, and though it often places foils that seem to reflect

Hannah's flaws back at her, they don't do much ultimately in terms of critique because Hannah and her voice are slow to change and quick to monopolize the screen.

During the fourth season, for example, Hannah briefly attends graduate school in Iowa. Her writing is so autobiographical that her classmates find it difficult to critique, and upon receiving those negative responses, Hannah forces her perspective on each of her classmates regarding the manifestations of their identities in their own creative writing. In doing so, Hannah embodies the complicated position of postfeminism – simultaneously representing *and* undermining feminist argument. When a male member accuses her of being hysterical, she pushes back against the misogynist foundations of the word. She retaliates, however, when a series of observations that are rooted in both racial and, most prominently, heteronormative stereotypes. When the tense situation comes to a head, Hannah quits the program, rejecting the institution that is rightly pushing back against her narcissistic worldview, an institution that also could have benefitted from the presence of a feminist voice.

Perhaps we as viewers are supposed to interpret this as folly, but without some deeper resolution, the plot upholds Hannah's commitment to operating as a free individual. Hannah is aware of feminism and utilizes its vocabulary but acts primarily to remove herself from the undesirable situation, as though simply leaving a "negative environment" is an appropriate or even viable solution. Clearly, she holds a privileged perspective, one that declines engagement rather than experiences personal discomfort. Hannah's empowerment arises in choosing herself. This commitment to individualism, rather than to contesting structures in the liberal feminist tradition, is further manifest in the "free woman's" experience of her empowered femininity through her female body.

The Free Woman's Body

Another quality of postfeminism, found in *Girls* is the focus on the exclusively female body as a source of empowerment (Adriaens). The show highlights and makes commentary on issues that are either exclusive to or primarily affect female bodies, as well as makes consistent choices surrounding the featuring of actresses bodies in ways that make their femaleness undeniable. In "All Adventurous Women Do" from the first season, Hannah's HPV diagnosis results in her confronting her current sexual partner, Adam, and her college boyfriend, Elijah (Andrew Rannells), to determine who gave her the infection. The discourse that surrounds HPV focuses on testing for Hannah – involving pap tests and cervical scraping with a direct focus on the physical reality of having a vagina – which contrasts with HPV's un-detectability in men. The episode concludes with Hannah embracing HPV as a marker of her empowered (sex) life, tweeting, "All adventurous women do." While the refusal to shy away from discussions of vagina and sexually transmitted infections is commendable, the ultimate argument of this episode is not that women face higher stigma regarding sex, promiscuity, and STIs, nor is it truly any kind of commentary on our discomfort with the female body and female sexuality; it is, instead, that all one has to do to be liberated from the anxiety surrounding sex and sexuality as a heterosexual woman is to be courageous and to own one's sexuality enough to vaguely tweet about it.

Another way *Girls* restricts empowerment exclusively to the female body is through the frequent exposure of Hannah's body, most frequently her breasts, but at times throughout the show her entire body is put on display. Throughout the series, Dunham has Hannah taking off her shirt on camera in both sexual and nonsexual situations. We see her body when she has sex and when she simply changes clothes alone in her apartment. One positive caveat concerning Dunham's treatment of these changing scenes is that, from what I perceive, they are not shot to cater to the male, sexualizing gaze. Such a tight focus on the bodies of the women throughout the show, however, moves us away from considering them and their experience of womanhood as defined by something other than their bodies, a theme that becomes more pronounced during the final season of the series when Hannah becomes pregnant from a brief affair with a man with whom she plans no continuing contact.

In "Bad Friend" from the second season, Hannah and Elijah use cocaine to fuel a night out at a club together as a way to inspire Hannah's freelance writing project. This episode features extended dance scenes in which Hannah is wearing nothing on her torso but a mesh tank top. In these scenes, Hannah is presented as free and empowered, if also high. The exposure of her breasts (of her explicitly female body) contributes to this aesthetic of freedom. In the episode "Hello Kitty" from the fifth season, Hannah is working as an English teacher after several bumps in the road of her never-quite-there writing career. She is reprimanded by the school's principal and, in what seems to be a panicked reaction to the potential of losing her job, flashes him her vagina *Basic Instinct* style to avoid disciplinary action. Dunham exposes her body in both instances as a power move of sorts. In both instances, however, her power and credibility are undermined: in the first, through her use of drugs and in the second, through the disagreement that Hannah and Fran have over her behavior.

Hannah is not the only character whose body contributes to manifest postfeminist perspective in *Girls*; Jessa embodies a Venus-like hyper-femininity, and her body (the sexuality that seems to permeate from her) often dominates the screen when Kirke is on camera. There are repeated references to Marnie, her conventional beauty, and the opportunities it affords her in both her personal and her professional life. Finally, and perhaps most interestingly, is the treatment of Shoshanna's virginity. In "She Did," Shoshanna and Ray have sex, which is the first time for Shoshanna. This event, along with the times in previous episodes that reference Shoshanna's virgin-status, is surrounded by a lot of rhetoric regarding Shoshanna's hymen. Much of that language comes from Shoshanna herself, and Ray takes this issue of being her first sexual partner very seriously. Shoshanna's first experience with sex is very tied to her female anatomy but marks her liberation and transition from a childlike status in relation to the other women to a full-fledged member of this sexually liberated cohort.

All in all, the show's focus on the explicit femaleness of its main characters operates similarly to its prioritizing of Hannah's narcissism: the corporeality of the empowerment represented in *Girls* moves the context of arguments for realized gender equity away from the societal, political, economic, or even intellectual structures that a) construct gender and b) uphold the oppressive and patriarchal systems that genuinely influence female-presenting bodies. This fixation on the free woman's body as a space of empowerment leads us to an analysis of the free woman's experience with sex.

The Free Woman's Desire

Sex is represented as consumerist – similarly to *Sex in the City* (Ross) – but also consumptive and integral to achieving personal pleasure, gratification, self-actualization, and autonomy. Much like the "limitless desire" Ross discusses in her chapter on *Sex in the City*, the sexual behaviors of the women on *Girls* are presented as pathways to agency (217). Sex is either an exercise in self-exploration, a utilization of another person for personal gratification, or an exhibition of liberation. Hannah, Marnie, and Shoshanna all, at times, explore themselves and discover and negotiate their own personal satisfaction in their sex lives. Hannah's sexual relationship with Adam fluctuates through several purposes: self-validation, social and sexual boundary-pushing, and gratification. Ultimately, however, the couple's sex life is most edifying for Hannah when it takes the form of a heteronormative, monogamous relationship. During the third season in an episode entitled "Role Play," Hannah attempts to reinstate the deviant sexuality that their relationship was founded on and, in doing so, drives a wedge between her and Adam that contributes to the demise of their relationship. Mirroring the white-knight trope that Adam has embodied in other ways for Hannah, the relegation of their sex life as something that "works" in the heteronormative, monogamous, appropriate sphere and reemphasizes a need for traditional gender behavior, should these women ever want to be happy.

Shoshanna, after her breakup with Ray, dives head first into the example set by her friends of using sex as a means of self-exploration. At a dinner party at Hannah's apartment in "It's a Shame About Ray," she explains her senior year plan of "alternating nights of [sexual] freedom with academic focus." Hannah declares it to be "smart, and strong, and feminist." Here, the show's script outright aligns feminism with sexual promiscuity for the sake of independence. This plan ends up having a negative influence on Shoshanna, however, when she lacks three credits required for her to walk across the stage at graduation, and she ends up lonely and unfulfilled, eventually crawling back to Ray and begging him to take her back. Had Shoshanna learned some sort of lesson regarding liberation from means other than sexual gratification, perhaps the plot could be argued to push back against this shallow, postfeminist vision of female empowerment. The result, though, is that Shoshanna desires the monogamous relationship she once had, further underscoring women's inability to "have-it-all" without a man.

Sex is not the only desire presented as simultaneously empowering and destructive. The show's relationship with food – particularly Hannah's constant eating and its contexts – illustrates a similar, underlying assumption that women's natural tendency is toward over- and unbridled consumption (Dejmanee). In fact, the show's pilot episode opens on a shot of Hannah with her mouth overflowing with pasta. Dejmanee argues that this is indicative of Hannah's determination to take any advantage given to her (127). This is a consistent behavior for Hannah. In "Free Snacks," Hannah begins a new job in advertising at GQ Magazine. She arrives at her first meeting with snacks spilling out of her arms as she discovers that the break room is stocked with complimentary snacks. While the show should be commended for showing women eating in a way that does not glorify diet culture, Hannah's apparent inability to contain her appetite and consumption of food leans on a longstanding trope that women lack self-control in general, and have incorrigible metaphorical appetites in terms of trying to fill a never-ending lack (Dejmanee). This lack of self-control manifests itself in Jessa's drug habit as well as Marnie's consistent sexual infidelities. All in all, the characters in *Girls* face more problems than praise for their desire, and the show falls prey to the oldest of female stereotypes: if the fruit is there for the picking, women just cannot help themselves.

Implications

Lena Dunham is quite frequently associated with, and actively links herself with, feminism. She is the co-creator of Lenny Letter, an e-newsletter that, among "style, health, politics, and everything else" names feminism as its foremost topic. Were it not for this fact, perhaps critics of *Girls* would take the problematic plotlines and misogynist tropes with a tiny grain of salt and chalk it up to an uninformed artist while adding the series to their list of modern sitcoms that, when it comes to gendered stereotypes, aren't quite as modern as we thought. Dunham is not, however, just some uninformed artist. She claims feminism and, therefore, her nearly autobiographical work is aligned with feminism. For proponents of an intersectional, politically active feminism, this is a problem. Postfeminist media masquerading as feminism is missing out on an opportunity to educate its viewership on the real issues feminism looks to address; or worse, it is actively misinforming viewers about what it means to hold feminist ideals.

The series finale of *Girls*, entitled "Latching," is a fitting end to the story of Hannah and her friends, if only because it's as complicated and frequently frustrating as the rest of the series. Having moved into a cute, Upstate home with Marnie to raise her newborn child, Hannah is predictably a mess. Unable to get her son, Grover, to latch and breastfeed, Hannah spirals back into self-pity and a dependent-yet-emotionally-abusive relationship with Marnie (a relationship that Marnie, not incidentally, chooses to avoid taking responsibility for her own life). She's only allowed her moment of clarity by the one-two punch of her mother's wisdom and an encounter with a runaway teen who, pants-less and overdramatic, forces Hannah to face a mirror to her own relentless self-absorption. After giving the girl her pants and shoes, Hannah walks home to her mother, her best friend, and (soon) a crying child. Ascending the stairs to his bedroom, she takes Grover into her arms and successfully nurses him. She is happy.

After years of pushing back and crawling forward and attempting to assert her independence from parents, men, and friends, it is in this blissful scene of domesticity that Hannah finds her adulthood. And, while motherhood is not anti-feminist – it's complicated and, in fact, necessary for human survival – this episode frames motherhood as the ultimate and inevitable resting place for the wild woman. It is problematic that Hannah's problems are solved and narrative closure is achieved by giving in to this domestic space, and the resolution is a bit pat that viewers finally see the protagonist as an adult when Grover successfully latches. While Hannah did not end up finding herself through a relationship with a man, Dunham's choice to portray success for Hannah as relegated to the domestic sphere and dependent upon her ability to be comfortable in that role further negates an envisioning of women's ability to successfully navigate all spheres of life that feminism could garner access to for girls and women.

Girls is a product of female empowerment envisioned as an individually attained concept. Although some viewers may read characters on the series as stand-ins for real women, the show is not feasibly generalizable. This series is a long series of snapshots of four women in all their flawed, human glory. Try to apply *Girls* to what it must be like for all women, and you will certainly fail. The show is too White, too privileged, and not nearly political enough to speak for women or for feminism. To discard *Girls* as anti-feminist is far too simple, however. Postfeminism, as Gill notes, "is clearly a response to feminism" (163). Let's consider it a response but not a refutation. *Girls* exemplifies much of what proponents of gender equity demand of society: women with identities separate from men, imbued with full humanity, and possessing the opportunity for self-determination. Lena Dunham's creation, despite its problems, still brings forth an occasional sigh of relief from me as I am sometimes refreshed by her characters who, despite leaning on narrative tropes, consistently push back against the cookie-cutter, traditionally modest-yet beautiful leading ladies of film and television past. In the other moments, however, I am reminded that Dunham herself, when pushed to describe the second season on David Letterman, summed up the plot this way:

"All the girls get new boyfriends and all the boys get new girlfriends. And then we're just bringing the drama." Gill describes the complex nature of postfeminist "sensibility" as, "Feminist ideas are at the same time articulated and repudiated, expressed and disavowed. Its constructions of contemporary gender relations are profoundly contradictory." We see this in *Girls*, and we see the continued need for characters like Hannah Horvath to be given a space. At the same time, we also see that to ignore the structures and the systems that the "real" feminist movement works to undo is problematic because making the claim that solitary control and self-determination is insulated from the political is to achieve only a very shallow empowerment for a very small, and very White, group of women. That is no victory.

*13.2 Adam Driver as Adam Sackler and Lena Dunham as Hannah Horvath in Girls,
"Together"*

NURSE JACKIE: THE COMPARTMENTALIZATION OF
MIDDLE ADULTHOOD

Katie Thevenow

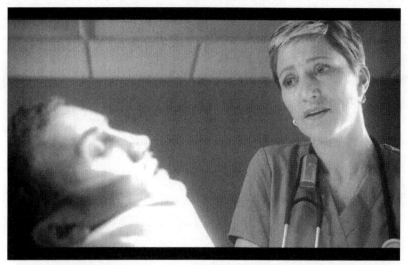

14.1 Edie Falco as Jackie Peyton in Nurse Jackie. "Sweet-N-All"

The Showtime series *Nurse Jackie* (2009-2015) centers on ER nurse Jackie Peyton (Edie Falco), who leads the nursing staff at All Saints Hospital in New York City. Jackie is a skilled nurse who goes out of her way to care for patients, but no one in the ER or in her personal life realizes that she accomplishes all of this with help from a secret drug addiction. Jackie's ambivalence about life, often expressed as behaviors and emotional detachment from the feelings of others, is demonstrated repeatedly over the run of the series as she does whatever it takes to manage the outcomes she wants with regard to her family relationships, work obligations, and (at times) elements in her personal life. Aside from having a penchant for Vicodin, Jackie also displays a fondness for debauchery of various sorts. This is aptly demonstrated in the direct line Jackie draws separating her professional persona and her life at home with her family. None of her coworkers, aside from her best friend Dr. Eleanor O'Hara (Eve Best), know that Jackie is married, has two children, and is having an affair with Eddie (Paul Schulze), the ER pharmacist. Jackie operates under her own moral code and redefines the traditional work-life balance of middle adulthood for straight, White females. Instead of finding a work-life balance, Jackie compartmentalizes her life, a structure she maintains regardless of the costs. This compartmentalization is demonstrated further as Jackie manipulates the steps of addiction recovery for her own benefit. The period of midlife is often characterized by stability, but Jackie's addiction only brings instability to her and the people who love her. Therefore, Jackie's character highlights, in glaringly obvious ways, the detrimental effects on a person's midlife when compartmentalization is used as a defense mechanism to keep the line drawn separating work life and personal life.

In the pilot episode of *Nurse Jackie*, Jackie shows viewers her façade, which gives them an inkling that she has figured out how to manage the various spheres of her middle adulthood – nursing work at the hospital, family life at home, and secret personal life in various spaces – while snorting prescription pain pills to keep the spheres of experience and relationship distinct and, for awhile at least, intact. Jackie begins her shift at All Saints Hospital by snorting a line in the bathroom. When a bike messenger is brought to the ER, Jackie checks the patient and realizes the man most likely has a brain bleed and needs a scan. Jackie relays this information to Dr. Fitch Cooper (Peter Facinelli), who ignores Jackie's request for the test. The bike messenger dies because Dr. Cooper never checks for a brain bleed. Albeit Jackie is a nurse and Dr. Cooper serves as her superior, but she makes the decision to chew out Dr. Cooper for his negligence and disregard for her medical suggestion and does not face any repercussions for insubordination. Jackie reveals a glimpse of her personal life to viewers when she gets a moment alone with Eddie. From their interaction, viewers learn that Jackie and Eddie are having a relationship and keeping it secret from other staffers at the hospital. Not insignificantly, Eddie also supplies Jackie with Oxycodone when she complains of back pain. As Jackie finishes her shift, she meets with Eddie outside of the hospital. She declines his request to accompany him to his place, and the two exchange "I love yous" before going their separate ways. As Jackie enters her home, viewers get their first inklings that Jackie has a family. She walks into the house and is greeted by two young girls, both of whom are happy to see her. Jackie then slips a ring on her left hand before walking through the kitchen to be greeted by a man who has made pancakes for dinner. From this commonplace, domestic interaction, viewers understand that Jackie actually has her own family, a husband and two daughters, outside of work. The first episode then ends with a voiceover (suggesting internal dialogue) of Jackie asking, "Make me good, God, but not yet,"

As seasons of *Nurse Jackie* unfold, the apparent ease of Jackie's compartmentalization becomes more complicated as viewers watch as the eponymous character struggle to maintain the separations she constructs and enforces among the three main spheres of her life. For most people, there is the public and private, professional and personal, which are relatively easy to label and describe. For Jackie, there is work and family and addiction, but in key ways all of the spheres contain secrets, which makes the usual bifurcation of what is public and what is private useless. In the latter part of the second season, Jackie uses a patient's MRI as her own to show her friend Dr. O'Hara that she is in pain and needs a prescription for more pills. After Jackie leaves, Dr. O'Hara proceeds to berate the hospital staff for not helping Jackie more at work after her injury. The workers then tell O'Hara that there is no patient named Jackie Peyton in the system. Jackie has lied to O'Hara in order to fuel her addiction. Meanwhile, on Jackie's way home after a shift, she encounters a woman who needs help because her boyfriend has had a seizure. Jackie attends to the man while waiting for the ambulance. During this time, Jackie notices the man has numerous baggies of pills in his pockets. She tells the girlfriend to back away from the man and proceeds to take the baggies and put them in her own pockets. When the ambulance arrives on the scene, Jackie tells emergency medical staffers to take the man to Bellevue Hospital instead of All Saints.

Viewers start to see more complications arise from the secrets Jackie keeps. When she walks into work, O'Hara is waiting for her. After avoiding O'Hara, Jackie realizes that the man she stole the pills from is in the waiting room of the hospital. Jackie then hides in the bathroom and calls her husband Kevin (Dominic Fumusa) to come pick her up. After leaving work early to avoid her problems, Jackie begins a weekend getaway with her husband and daughters. As the family is settling into a bed and breakfast for the night, however, Jackie abruptly ends the vacation when she realizes she cannot find her pills. For the first time, viewers begin to realize that despite her competence in the ER and maneuvers to keep the different areas of her life distinct Jackie cannot function without her pills. Actually, everything is a struggle for Jackie – she struggles with the divide between her work and family life, and she also struggles to satisfy her addiction.   During the finale of the second season, viewers notice a break in Jackie's character when she appears to make herself vulnerable with Kevin. The emotional opening occurs after Kevin has discovered that Jackie agreed to take a sum of money from O'Hara after Jackie swore to Kevin she would not take the money. It is unclear, however, whether her emotional conversation with Kevin is authentic or just another managing technique to keep a compartment of her life intact.

Jackie: (Teary-eyed) I'm not here – not the way you are. When they fall down, they run to you. There are days when I look at them and I think, you know, what the fuck? I gave birth to you – and I fucking hate myself for being so selfish and for being competitive. You keep saying we don't need anybody's help, we're fine, but I don't have that peace of mind that you do Kevin. And I'm fucking jealous that you can sleep at night. Yes, I took the money and I'm sorry but I did it to help us, not to rip us apart.

After her emotional pleas, it appears that Kevin has been successfully managed and that Jackie is able to regain control of her family life.

Relative calm is short-lived, however. Jackie's control is undermined when Kevin discovers a key to a separate mailbox belonging to Jackie. Inside the mailbox, he discovers credit card statements with charges from numerous pharmacies throughout the city. Kevin then consults Jackie's friend, Dr. O'Hara, and together they come to the understanding that Jackie has a drug problem. The same day Jackie returns home from work to find Kevin and Dr. O'Hara waiting for her.

Jackie: What's up? Where are the girls?

Kevin: Let's just sit down for a minute.

Jackie: Oh. Oh no. No, no, no, no. No, no, no, no, no fucking way.

O'Hara: It's okay, Jacks.

Jackie: On, no, no, way. You have to leave right now, I'm sorry. Where are the girls?

195

Kevin:	My sister's, and I asked her to come, okay?
Jackie:	You are fucking hilarious. (To O'Hara) He fucking hates your guts. (To Kevin) You hate her guts. You invited her all the way out here to Queens to fucking gossip about me?
O'Hara:	This isn't what this is about.
Jackie:	(Angrily) You think anybody wants to listen to what you have to fuckin' say about this?
Kevin:	You're a drug addict.
Jackie:	And you're a fucking idiot! You have no idea what you're talking about.

As an intervention is attempted, Jackie retreats to the bathroom and locks herself inside. Jackie looks in the mirror and imagines admitting that she is a drug addict. After this reasonable projection, Jackie returns to reality by laughing and saying, "blow me." Jackie does anything to avoid the negative attribute of labeling herself as a drug addict. The denial of this claim perfectly demonstrates her usage of compartmentalization (Thomas, Ditzfield, and Showers 719). Jackie tries her hardest to manage her compartments because the management aids in protecting Jackie Peyton's main focus: her addiction. By maintaining her image as a competent nurse, loving mom, and devoted wife, Jackie uses compartmentalization as a defense mechanism; it is effective (for a period of time) for hiding her addiction, and compartmentalization also allows Jackie to defend her actions and avoid negative self-beliefs (Thomas, et al. 719).

Addicts are not associated with any particular stage of life because addiction can happen at any time. Jackie, as a character, offers viewers a perspective on addiction from the standpoint of midlife. Looking across the human lifespan, midlife is characterized by higher levels of martial satisfaction, better life satisfaction, and mastery than is found among younger individuals (Keyes and Ryff 719-727), and midlife is also associated with overall good health (Merrill and Verbrugge 78). Midlife is significant because it offers the ideal timeframe for achieving a balance between work and home. In contrast, popular media texts are built around conflict, which is the classical narrative paradigm dating back at least to Aristotle. This being the case, it is not surprising that women in situation comedies often must continually negotiate between containment in the home and their own independence (Mellencamp 80-95). When taking the characteristics of midlife at face value, Jackie would appear to be positioned for the ideal representation of midlife. As Jackie's addiction affects how she manages her compartments, however, a chain reaction occurs that starts to destroy her overall stability (not to mention damaging all of the people close to her). Viewers observe this instability begin to root with the attempt at intervention undertaken by Kevin and Dr. O'Hara. Instead of trying to achieve a traditional work and home binary, Jackie continues to negotiate and manage the challenges of her two entirely different worlds. She tries her hardest to keep her family a secret from her coworkers, her affair a secret from her family and coworkers, and her drug addiction a secret from every person in her life. Of course, given the demands of traditional narrative structure – the saying "drama is conflict" is overarching and refers to comedy as well – it is not surprising that collisions of Jackie's private and public spheres begin to take place with increasing regularity. One such collision occurs when Kevin comes to the hospital for the first time. He is greeted by Jackie's student nurse, Zoey Barkow (Merritt Wever), and asks to see Jackie Peyton. When Kevin says he is her husband, Zoey says that is impossible because Jackie is not married. Other of Jackie's spheres collide when Eddie befriends Kevin after discovering he is Jackie's husband. Much to Jackie's surprise (and to her satisfaction), Eddie does not tell Kevin about the affair. Against Jackie's wishes, however, Eddie continues the friendship.

Jackie appears to manage her interactions in the public sphere much successfully and for a longer period of time than she manages her life in the private sphere. While she has been able to keep her addiction a secret from her colleagues longer than from her husband and best friend, Jackie falters in the third season of the series when she steals drugs from the Oncology Department for her personal use. Jackie's boss, Gloria Akalitus (Anna Deavere Smith), places Jackie on probation after discovering the source of the missing drugs. Furthermore, a bigger collision occurs when Kevin shows up at the hospital with their daughters. Jackie's strict distinction between her public and private spheres has started to fade. Jackie fears what she considers the worst outcome, that her compartmentalizing has failed and her husband knows about Jackie's affair with Eddie, but instead, Kevin confesses to Jackie that he has had an affair with another woman.

> Kevin: I fucked up. It's over. It will never happen again. You gotta believe me Jackie. Believe me.
>
> Jackie: Wha-what am I supposed to say?
>
> Kevin: I don't know: I love you? I forgive you? Something like that.
>
> Jackie: Pack your bags.

With Kevin out of the house and Jackie's desperation growing to feed her addiction, she takes home a stranger to do drugs. When the man overdoses and dies in Jackie's house, she relies on Dr. O'Hara to help with reporting the overdosed stranger as a man she found dead on the street. After this, it appears that Jackie is ready to admit she needs professional when she confides in Dr. O'Hara that she thinks she needs to go to rehab. It would seem Jackie is genuine in her cry for help, and she does start a 28-day rehab program. Unfortunately, it isn't long before her self-destructive tendencies take over, and Jackie begins to compartmentalize during rehab. She convinces herself that she can complete the program in half the time and subsequently leaves after two weeks.

Throughout the seven seasons of *Nurse Jackie*, viewers notice a lack of transparency that, at times, makes it difficult to understand Jackie's motivations. After Kevin discovers Jackie has been in rehab, he files for divorce, which brings more instability into her middle adulthood. Jackie meets a guy who cares about her, but she cheats on him with a younger drug dealer. Her self-destructive tendencies reinforce her need for compartmentalization as a maintenance strategy. Her best friend pays for her rehab, but she leaves early and does not stay sober. She gets a supportive, 12-step sponsor, but is threatened by the fact that the sponsor knows Jackie is still using, so Jackie uses a ruse to send her sponsor into rehab in Jackie's place. She convinces a dying nun to take the blame for illegal prescriptions Jackie had filled so the nurse avoids getting into trouble. She begins using pills again on the one-year anniversary of her sobriety. Most of the time, Jackie shows no remorse for the decisions she makes while following her own moral code even though she damages first her domestic relationships then her professional relationships. By prioritizing her needs over everyone and everything else, and with her need to conceal her addiction at the center of it all, Jackie rejects the notion of transparency that is typical of a female protagonist in a situation comedy, which is great for the series in terms of dramatic opportunity but – for viewers who empathize with Jackie – far from positive for the character (Subramanian 215).

The lack of transparency in Jackie's character advances the idea that *Nurse Jackie* is not a conventional sitcom. Although the show focuses the narrative on a female protagonist, and viewers have certain gendered expectations about what such stories should look like, Jackie is not always a likeable character. After all, she creates her own moral code constructed to maximize professional and personal gain. She prioritizes her addiction over her family and her job. Jackie draws distinct lines separating each sphere of her life, and her self-destructive tendencies are far more likely to leave viewers far crying instead of laughing. This unconventional sitcom still draws on certain conventions of the sitcom genre, however. *Nurse Jackie* is a half-hour, single camera narrative although it fits more as a "dramedy" in tone (Subramanian 212). The 30-minute show features aspects of dark comedy and provides a dramatic narrative of a female protagonist limited by a very real drug addiction. Overall, the series offers an original interpretation of the sitcom genre. While conforming to the structure and aesthetics of a traditional sitcom, the context of the show diverges from the conventions of the typical sitcom. As Jackie eschews the typical sitcom morality of a female protagonist in middle adulthood (Subramanian 219), viewers are often left with the question of whether or not to root for Jackie. Viewer response to Jackie is mediated by one particular character throughout the series. As Zoey Barkow weaves in and out of Jackie's personal and professional lives, she offers a measure of how viewers are likely to feel about Jackie over the course of the series. When Zoey first meets Jackie, she idolizes her. She follows Jackie throughout work taking notes on her nursing techniques. She respects Jackie as a nurse and then later as a mom. Zoey runs interference for Jackie with her kids and, at one point, even becomes Jackie's roommate. Furthermore, she covers for Jackie and makes excuses for her. It is a fair assessment to argue that Zoey becomes Jackie's biggest fan. Zoey's character shows her most significant role in the series – not to mention her greatest personal growth in terms of character arc – by finally giving up on her friend, which demonstrates the extremity of the effects of Jackie's compartmentalization.

During the sixth season, Jackie convinces a dying nun to take the blame for illegal prescriptions Jackie had been filling by creating a fake ID for her. After the nun dies, Zoey realizes what Jackie has done. She confides in their boss that she believes Jackie is using again, which results in Jackie having to take a drug test. Jackie then confronts Zoey.

Zoey: You used a picture of a dying nun to make a fake ID.

Jackie: Listen, Zoey...

Zoey: And then you convinced her the very last thing she did on Earth-- to lie for you and say that she was Nancy Wood and that she stole Carrie's DEA number.

Jackie: Ok, listen, I can—this has got to be hard for you.

Zoey: What's hard for me is that you've been using this whole time.

Jackie: I can see that you—that that's maybe what you're thinking right now.

Zoey: You stole a DEA number. That's a federal offense. You can go to jail. If you don't go to rehab, I will hand the picture over.

Jackie now faces an important decision: will she enter a diversion program, which would allow her to keep her nursing license but requires that she self-admit to using drugs; or will she take a drug test and risk losing her license. Jackie's management system has failed her, but her judgment is clouded by her addiction and the fact that she has sometimes eluded detection and consequences in the past. When confronted by two paths that she finds equally unappealing, Jackie refuses to admit defeat and chooses neither option.

With help from her remaining supporter, Eddie, Jackie decides to leave New York with an abundance of pills and go to Florida. Her irrational, last-minute escape plan fails when Jackie gets into a car accident and the police discover her plethora of pills in her vehicle. Her escape attempt epitomizes the unconventionality of Jackie's middle adulthood because she has chosen herself and her addiction above all else. She has disregarded the notion integrating the private and public spheres of her life and choosing what is best for her two daughters as well as for her career. Instead, she chooses to abandon any and all stability in her life by pretending her problems do not exist (another way of compartmentalizing) and going to Florida because, in her mind, this is Jackie's last possible way to privilege her drug addiction over the other spheres. Compartmentalization allows the avoidance of negative self-attributes (Thomas, et al. 729). Jackie is willing to leave her job and family behind before admitting that she is using drugs to her coworkers. Midlife is characterized by a period of emotional stability with an ideal work-life balance (Kessler, Foster, Webster, and House 310-311), but Jackie can no longer relate to either of these aspects of her life, both of which were once very important to her. Instead, Jackie is forced to reconfigure her compartmentalization when she is jailed after the accident because of the possession of the pills. After going through a forced detox, Jackie is released from jail and uses this opportunity to her advantage. Instead of telling her family she was in jail, she tells them she had been in rehab. Finally, her work conflict cannot be compartmentalized, and she is left with no choice but to enter the diversion program. After being stripped from the majority of her nursing duties, she becomes focused and determined to keep her nursing license and her job.

Gloria:	Don't celebrate too soon Jackie, diversion is gonna be hell. You may not touch patients, and just so nobody mistakes you for a real nurse lose the blue scrubs.
Jackie:	Deal.

In one of the most significant signs of the detrimental effects compartmentalization, and thus addiction, has on Jackie, Zoey is assigned to be Jackie's monitor during diversion. Zoey now has to make sure Jackie completes a checklist of nursing assistant duties and complies with a drug test every day.

This role reversal is profound and signifies the realism of the consequences Jackie has brought onto herself, but Jackie manages to complete the diversion program and keep her nursing license. She has been given the benefit of the doubt one last time and manages to regain control of her career. But, true to her history as a character on the series, Jackie soon returns to old patterns: she compartmentalizes her job and begins using drugs again. During the intervening time, however, All Saints has been purchased by a developer and will no longer remain a hospital. Jackie's longstanding nursing career provides her with an opportunity to work at another hospital, and Jackie asks Zoey to join her in this new chapter in her professional life.

Jackie:	Are you coming to Bellevue with me?
Zoey:	I need to move on, and I need you to let me.
Jackie:	We can move on together, Zoey. When I first met you, you were wearing bunny scrubs and now you're head nurse.
Zoey:	I know, the first time I met you I was afraid of you. And it's just then I wanted to be you. And now all I do is worry about you.

Zoey's refusal of Jackie's offer is significant in that it demonstrates Jackie can no longer maintain the level of compartmentalization she once had. Jackie believes Zoey will come with her and counts on that, but Zoey has realized that she needs to move away from Jackie. As Zoey continues to serve as a conduit for viewers' perceptions of Jackie, this shift invites viewers to change their allegiance away from Jackie's character. Even though Jackie has managed to salvage her career one more time, the road has been rocky and trust in her as eroded, which creates distance between Jackie and everyone in her life. Perhaps it is this distance that keeps her coworkers from realizing that Jackie started using drugs immediately after regaining her job and her license to practice nursing. This seems a believable and fitting way to wind the series down; just as Zoey is ready to move on and get on with her life, viewers of *Nurse Jackie* are ready to move on, too, because there is nowhere left to accompany a character that refuses to end her addiction or to finally come clean about who she is.

In the series finale of *Nurse Jackie*, the sale of the hospital is final, and staff members celebrate their last time together in that space. True to form, Jackie takes a heaping dose of drugs in the bathroom during the party. Jackie is then shown leaving the hospital and walking around New York City. This ephemeral journey is brought back to reality, however, when Jackie's coworkers discover her unconscious on the floor. Zoey comforts her friend one last time, "You're good, Jackie. You're good. You're good." The camera pulls out on Jackie, revealing her stretched out on the floor and surrounded by her coworkers. With this, the series concludes, leaving viewers to determine if Jackie dies from the overdose or is revived. At minimum, Jackie has been caught using at the hospital for the last time and can no longer rely on the benefit of the doubt, which has given her a great deal of benefit over the years. Her compartmentalization has attained the ultimate consequence for Jackie: she has now lost everything she has worked for so diligently. The open-ended nature of the series leaves room for viewers to speculate. Zoey's dialogue offers significance in its similarity to Jackie's lines at the beginning of the series. The pilot episode of the series ends with a voiceover of Jackie asking, "Make me good, God, but not yet." The significance of this dialogue is brought to light when the time arrives for Jackie to be "made good." The sitcom *Nurse Jackie* shows that a female protagonist does not have to follow a traditional mold of middle adulthood for heterosexual, White women, which is the dominant mode of representation for them on television. Instead of achieving a balance between work and life, Jackie compartmentalizes the spheres of her life and follows her own moral code. Her main source of motivation is her addiction, which means she must keep her work and personal lives separate in order to better protect the secret addiction. Jackie continually faces the challenge of managing two different worlds. Her compartmentalization keeps her from achieving recovery because she never believes she needs to recover. Jackie is a vivid example of what can happen when compartmentalizing is used as a defense mechanism. The most important aspect of this defense mechanism is that it is used, in part, to help hide her addiction. Because Jackie never ends up staying sober, this failure demonstrates the negative effect compartmentalization can have and explains why her complete recovery was never possible. The direct line drawn to separate different spheres of her life tricks Jackie into thinking she is always in control when, in fact, she never was. As a result, Jackie ends up losing everything.

CONTRIBUTORS

ELYSE CONKLIN is a sardonic Chicagoan, and her favorite TV show is *Veronica Mars*. Her research interests include critical economic theory, Marxist feminism, and critical legal studies. Her masters in Communication Studies thesis is titled "Striking the Match: A Rhetorical Analysis of the 2012 Chicago Teachers Strike."

SERENA DAYA is a two-time graduate of Wake Forest University, earning a M.A. and B.A. in Communication. She will pursue her Ph.D in Communication at the University of Kentucky. She's probably related to Aziz Ansari because...aren't we all?

MAX DOSSER exists and appears in this volume. Though one day, only one of those things will be true. Max has called Wake Forest University home for seven years, and there he received a B.A. in Chemistry, a second B.A. in Music in Liberal Arts, and an M.A. in Communication. After he graduates, he will pursue an M.F.A. in Filmmaking.

COURTNEY GREEN is a graduate of Butler University but born and raised in Columbus, Ohio. She is currently pursuing her M.A. at Wake Forest University and is interested in examining the relationship African-American college students have with microaggressions while studying at a predominately white institution.

LEAH HAYNES will beat you at Harry Potter trivia. "Always." A word nerd, soccer lover, and "Double Deac," she earned her B.A. in English and Communication in 2016 and her M.A. in Communication in 2017, both from Wake Forest University. Her current research interests include the intersections of feminism, health, narrativity, gender, and The South, but she's also been known to write on T.S. Eliot's *The Wasteland* (a wonderful English thesis, in fact, that's diligently gathering dust on her parents' shelves).

KRISTINA KOKKONOS is a Beyoncé expert, a real cheese lover, a friggin Tar Heel, and an avid Oxford comma hater.

KATIE NELSON is Southern girl glad to be back in the South. She is a graduate of Bates College in frigid Lewiston, Maine and currently a masters student at Wake Forest University writing about body image and the impossibility of perfection. Following graduation, Katie will pursue her Ph.D. in Communication at Louisiana State University.

KEVIN PABST is a graduate of The University of Alabama where he learned to master the phrase "Roll Tide." He currently writes about cartoons while pursuing his M.A. at Wake Forest University and will teach for Duke Talent Identification Program once he graduates. Roll Tide.

SAMANTHA RIPPETOE is a graduate of Humboldt State University and is now completing her M.A. at Wake Forest University in Communication. She has recently accepted to attend the University of Georgia to achieve her Ph.D. Her interests in academia are centered around gender and argumentation, and she not only uses these skills in her scholarship but also as an assistant coach of the Wake Forest Debate Team. Though school fills up most of her time, the remainder of it is filled up by her large and loud cat, Kyle, who is not afraid to use his girth or voice to get what he wants: pets.

CALLIE SARTAIN After attending prom with national football champion Deshaun Watson, Callie received a B.A. in Communication Studies and Spanish from Mercer University. She is a current M.A. student at Wake Forest University with interests in reproductive rights, health communication, and anything Foucault. Following graduation, Callie will take a nice long nap and maybe pursue a Ph.D.

JENN ST SUME is a second year M.A. student in the Communication Department. Her research focuses on the function of race, narrative, and political communication throughout the Obama administration. Over the summer, she worked as the Dorm Director of the Ben Franklin Transatlantic Fellows Program, a U.S. State Department grant initiative that educates high school students about international diplomacy and relations. She earned her B. A. in Communication from Florida Atlantic University where she also served as Co-Captain of their Division I Women's Volleyball team.

KAROLINE SUMMERVILLE is a true nerd who hoards words in the form of books and laughs too hard at jokes. She received her B.A. in Communication from Queens University of Charlotte and is finishing up her M.A. at Wake Forest University. She plans to eat as much mint chocolate chip ice cream as she can while she pursues her lifelong goal of obtaining her doctorate.

KATIE THEVENOW is a graduate of Butler University and enjoys spending time with her friends, family, and her two dogs: Grizzly and Bailey. After finishing her M.A. at Wake Forest University, she looks forward to relocating back to her family farm in Indiana to spend time with her beloved pony, Lil' Sebastian. She fully acknowledges that her last name looks like a typo but can assure you it is not.

COREY WASHBURN is a "Double Deac," graduating from Wake Forest University with a B.A. in English in 2016 and with her M.A. in Communication in 2017. Following graduation, she plans to work for a startup marketing firm in Winston-Salem and to pursue entrepreneurship through digital media for Shark Tank entrepreneurs.

WORKS CITED

Ahmed, Sara. "Happy Objects." *The Affect Theory Reader*. By Melissa Gregg and Gregory J. Seigworth. North Carolina: Duke UP, 2011. N. pag. Print.

Althusser, Louis. *Essays on Ideology*. London: Verso, 1993. Print.

Andrews, John. "Daria the Untold Tale." Weblog post. *The Huffington Post*, 10 June 2014.

Arrested Development. FOX. 02 November 2003. Television.

Arrested Development. Netflix. 26 May 2013. Television.

Artt, Sarah, and Anne Schwan. "Screening Women's Imprisonment Agency and Exploitation in Orange Is the New Black." *Television & New Media* 17.6 (2016): 467–472. *tvn.sagepub.com*. Web.

Auslander, Philip. "Liveness: Performance and the Anxiety of Simulation." *Performance and Cultural Politics*. London: Routledge, 1996. N. pag. Print.

Baltes, Paul B. "Theoretical Propositions of Life-Span Developmental Psychology on the Dynamics Between Growth and Decline." *Developmental Psychology*, vol. 23, no. 5, pp. 611-26.

Baudrillard, Jean. *The Ecstasy of Communication*. Cambridge, MA: Semiotext(e), 2012. Print.

--. *Simulacra and Simulation*. Ann Arbor: U of Michigan, 1994. Print.

Bednarek, Monika. "'Wicked' Women In Contemporary Pop Culture: 'Bad' Language And Gender In *Weeds*, *Nurse Jackie*, And *Saving Grace*." *Text & Talk* 35.4 (2015): 431-451.

Berlant, Lauren Gail. *Cruel Optimism*. Durham: Duke UP, 2011. Print.

Bicchieri, Cristina. *The Grammar of Society: The Nature and Dynamics of Social Norms*.

Birthisel, Jessica, and Jason A. Martin. ""That's What She Said":
     Gender, Satire, And The   American Workplace On The
     Sitcom *The Office.*" *Journal Of Communication Inquiry* 37.1
     (2013): 64-80. Communication & Mass Media Complete.
     Web. 31 Oct. 2016.

Blair, C., Jeppeson, M. S., & Pucci, E., Jr. (1991). Public
     Memorializing in Postmodernity: The Vietnam Veterans
     Memorial as Prototype. *The Quarterly Journal of Speech*, 77(3),
     263.

Blake, Aaron. "Donald Trump's Amazing Answer to 'Do You
     Cry?'" *Washington Post.* N.p., 19Jan. 2016. Web. 18 Dec.
     2016.

Bob-Waksberg, Raphael. "Q&A: The Creator of *BoJack Horseman*
     Discusses the Comedy of Depression and the 'Bill Cosby
     Episode.'" Interview by Eric Thurm. *Grantland,*
     N.p., 4 Aug. 2015. Web. 18 Dec. 2016.

BoJack Horseman. Netflix. 22 August 2014. Television.

Braeden, Jen and Mary Dalton. "Jen Braeden on Sitcom Writing."
     Vimeo,   uploaded   at
     https://build.zsr.wfu.edu/sitcomreader/watch/jen-
     braeden-on-sitcom-writing

Burke, Kenneth and Gusfield, Joseph R. *On Symbols and Society.*
     Chicago: University of Chicago Press, 1989. Print.

Burke, Kenneth. *A Rhetoric of Motives.* Berkeley: University of
     California Press, 1969. Print.

Burke, Kenneth. *A Grammar of Motive.* University of California
     Press, 1969. Cambridge University Press, 2005. Print.

Chappell, Les. "*BoJack Horseman* rides into season three atop the
     Secretariat Oscar campaign." *The A.V. Club.* N.p., 22 July
     2016. Web. 18 Dec. 2016.

Cohen, Ira. J. and Robert Antonio. *Marx and Modernity: Key Readings
     and Commentary* (1st ed.). GB: Wiley-Blackwell, 2003. Print.

Collins, Jim. "Television and Postmodernism." Ed. Paul Marris and Sue Thornham. *Media Studies: A Reader.* New York: New York UP, 2000. N. pag. Print.

Communication & Mass Media Complete. Web. 31 Oct. 2016.

Community. NBC. 17 September 2009. Television.

Community. Yahoo! TV. 17 March 2015. Television.

Cruz, Lenika. "*Unbreakable Kimmy Schmidt* and the Sunny Side of Surviving." *The Atlantic* 3 Mar. 2015. *Theatlantic.com.* Web. 15 Nov. 2016.

Curnalia, Rebecca M. L. and Dorian L. Mermer. "The 'Ice Queen' Melted And It Won Her The Primary: Evidence Of Gender Stereotypes And The Double Bind In News Frames Of Hillary Clinton's 'Emotional Moment.'" *Qualitative Research Reports In Communication* 15.1 (2014): 26-32. Communication & Mass Media Complete. Web. 31 Oct. 2016.

Csikszentmihalyi, Mihaly. *Flow: The Psychology of Optimal Experience.* New York: Harper Perennial Modern Classics, 2009. Print.

D'Addario, Daniel. "*Master of None* Knows Exactly What It's Doing." *Time* 13 Nov. 2015. *time.com.* Web. 3 Nov. 2016.

Daria. MTV. 1997-2001. Television.

Dalton, Mary M. and Laura R. Linder. *The Sitcom Reader: America Re-viewed, Still Skewed.* SUNY Press, 2016.

Deleuze, Gilles, and Felix Guattari. *Anti-Oedipus: Capitalism and Schizophrenia.* Minneapolis: U of Minnesota, 1983. Print.

Dhaenens, Frederik and Van Bauwel, Sofia. "Queer Resistances in the Adult Animated Sitcom." *Television & New Media,* vol. 13, no. 2, 2012, pp. 124-138.

Epstein, Leonora. "6 Major Differences Between *Orange Is The New Black* The Book And TV Show." *BuzzFeed.* N.p., n.d. Web. 1 Nov. 2016.

Era of Reality TV, but Some Insist on Revival." *Advertising Age.* 75.18 (2004): S-34. *Academic Search Premier.* Web. 2 Nov 2016.

Fahrentold, David. "Trump Recorded Having Extremely Lewd Conversation about Women in 2005." *Washington Post.* N.p., 8 Oct. 2016. Web. 17 Dec. 2016.

Fejes, Fred and Kevin Petrich. "Invisibility, Homophobia and Heterosexism: Lesbians, Gays, and the Media." N.p., Dec. 1993. Web. 1 Nov. 2016.

Feltmate, David and Brackett, Kimberly, P. "A Mother's Value Lies in Her Sexuality: *The Simpsons, Family Guy,* and *South Park* and the Preservation of Traditional Sex Roles." *Symbolic Interaction*, vol. 37, no. 4, 2014, pp. 541-557.

Fisher, Carla L. and Canzona, Mollie Rose. "Interpersonal Communication Dynamics Among Providers and Older Adult Patients." *Health Care Interactions in Older Adulthood.* Eds. Nussbaum, Jon F. and Worthington, Amber. New York: 2014. 391-393. Print.

Foa, Edna B, and Barbara Olasov Rothbaum. *Treating the Trauma of Rape: Cognitive behavioral Therapy for PTSD.* Guilford Press, 2001. Print.

Foucault, Michel. "The Subject and Power." *Critical Inquiry* 8.4 (1982): 777–795. Print.

Frimberger, Katja. "A Brechtian Theatre Pedagogy for Intercultural Education Research." *Language & Intercultural Communication*, vol. 16 no. 2, May.2016, pp. 130-147.

Gilmore Girls. The WB. 5 October 2000. Television.

Gilmore Girls: A Year in the Life. 25 November 2016. Television.

Gonzalez, Briana. "19 Lesbian and Bisexual TV Shows and Movies You Should Already Be Watching." pride.com N.p., 30 Mar. 2015. Web. 1 Nov. 2016.

Goodman, Tim. "R.I.P., *Arrested Development* -- Critics' Fave Not Given Room to Grow."

Guggenheim, Lauren, Nojin Kwak, and Scott W. Campbell. "Nontraditional News Negativity: The Relationship of Entertaining Political News Use to Political Cynicism and Mistrust." *International Journal of Public Opinion Research* 23.3 (2011): 287–314. Print.

Heath, Stephen. *Questions of Cinema.* Bloomington: Indiana U, 2011. Print.

Holmes, Linda. "*Crazy Ex-Girlfriend*, Foolishness, Happiness And Josh Chan." *NPR*. NPR, 28 Mar. 2016. Web. 31 Mar. 2017.

Hornby, Richard. "The Decline of the American Musical Comedy." *The Hudson Review* 41.1 (1988): 182. Web.

Householder April Kalogeropoulos and Adrienne Trier-Bieniek. *EBL Reader - Feminist Perspectives on Orange Is the New Black : Thirteen Critical Essays.* N.p., 2016. Print.

Ivins-Hulley, Laura. "Narrowcasting Feminism: MTV's *Daria*." *The Journal of Popular Culture* 47.6 (2014): 1198-212. Web.

Johnson, Davi. "Mapping the Meme: A Geographical Approach to Materialist Rhetorical Criticism." *Communication and Critical/Cultural Studies* 4.1 (2007): 27-50. Web.

Kaplan, E. Ann. *Rocking around the Clock: Music Television, Postmodernism, and Consumer Culture.* New York: Methuen, 1987. Print.

Kellner, Douglas. *Media Culture: Cultural Studies, Identity, and Politics between the Modern and the Postmodern.* London ; New York: Routledge, 1995. Print.

Kelly, Stephen. "Depicting Depression: A Difficult Tale to Tell on TV." *The Independent.* N.p., 15 Nov. 2014. Web. 18 Dec. 2016.

Kennedy, Angie C. and Kristen A. Prock. "'I Still Feel Like I Am Not Normal': A Review of the Role of Stigma and

Stigmatization Among Female Survivors of Child Sexual Abuse, Sexual Assault, and Intimate Partner Violence." *Trauma Violence and Abuse* (2016). Print.

Kennedy, Tammie M. et al. "Whiteness Studies." *Rhetoric Review*, 24, 359-402, 2009. Web.

Kerman, Piper. *Orange Is the New Black: My Year in a Women's Prison.* Spiegel & Grau, 2011. Print.

Kidd, Briony. "Umbilical Fears: Jennifer Kent's *The Babadook.*" *Metro Magazine*, no. 180, 2014, 6-12.

Klein, Sarah. "What Neuroscience Has to Say About the 'Tortured Genius.'" *Huffington Post.* N.p., 2 Sep. 2014. 18 Dec. 2016. Web.

Kutulas, Judy. "Liberated Women and New Sensitive Men." *The Sitcom Reader: America Re-viewed, Still Skewed.* Eds. Mary M. Dalton and Laura R. Linder. New York: Suny Press, 2016. 121-132. Print.

---. "Who Rules the Roost?" *The Sitcom Reader: America Re-viewed, Still Skewed.* By Mary M. Dalton and Laura R. Linder. Albany: State U of New York, 2016. N. pag. Print.

Laclau, Ernesto, and Chantal Mouffe. *Hegemony and Socialist Strategy: Towards a Radical Democratic Politics.* London: Verso, 2014. Print.

Laughland, Oliver. "Donald Trump and the Central Park Five: The Racially Charged Rise of a   Demagogue." *The Guardian* 17 Feb. 2016. *The Guardian.* Web. 17 Dec. 2016.

Law, Larry. "Revolutionary Self-Theory." *Spectacular Times* (1985): n. pag. *Anarchist Library.* Web.

Lebowitz, Michael A. *Beyond Capital: Marx's Political Economy of the Working Class* (2nd;2; ed.). GB: Palgrave. 2003. Print.

Lee, Traci G. "*Master of None* Wins at Emmys, Celebrates Story of Immigrant Parents." *NBC News.* N.p., 19 Sept. 2016. Web. 19 Dec. 2016.

Lockenhoff, Corinna E. and Carstensen, Laura L. "Socioemotional Selectivity Theory, Aging, and Health: The Increasingly Delicate Balance Between Regulating Emotions and Making Tough Choices." *Journal of Personality* 72.6 (2004): 1395-1424. *Blackwell Publishing*. Web. 1 Nov. 2016.

Lowry, Brian. "Review: *Arrested Development*." *Variety*. Penske Business Media, 26 May 2013. Web. 12 December 2016.

Lubin, Gus. "How a Comedian With No Experience Got Such Huge Names to Join *BoJack Horseman*." *Business Insider*. N.p., 3 Oct. 2014. Web. 18 Dec. 2016.

Malone, Michael. "The Labor Pains Of Peak TV." *Broadcasting & Cable*. 146.16 (2016): 10-12. Print.

McCleland, Susan. (2016). Roseanne, *Roseanne*, reality, and domestic comedy. In Dalton, Mary M., and Laura R. Linder (Eds.), *The Sitcom Reader: America Re-viewed, Still Skewed* (Second ed.; 165-176). Albany: State University of New York Press.

McIntosh, P. (1989). "White Privilege: Unpacking the Invisible Knapsack." *Peace and Freedom Magazine*, 10-12.

"Misconceived At Others." *Hitfix*. Hitfix, 31 October 2016. Web. 29 May 2013.

Moylan, Brian. "*Louie* Isn't a Sitcom About Nothing – It's a Comedy About Everything." *The Guardian* 10 April 2015. Web 18 Dec. 2016.

Murthi, Vikram. "Absurdist Humor, Biting Drama Groom *BoJack Horseman* Into One of TV's Best Shows." *The A.V. Club*. N.p., 17 July 2015. Web. 18 Dec. 2016.

National Institute of Mental Health. "Health and Education." *NIMH*. N.p., 2015. Web. 18 Dec. 2016.

Newman, Kathy A. "'Misery Chick,' Irony, Alienation, and Animation in MTV's *Daria*." *Prime Time Animation: Television*

Animation and American Culture. Carol A. Stabile and Mark Harrison (eds.). London: Routledge, 2003. N. pag. Print.

Nussbaum, Emily. "The Bleakness and Joy of *BoJack Horseman.*" *The New Yorker.* N.p., 8 Aug. 2016. Web. 18 Dec. 2016.

Odd Mom Out. BravoTV. 08 June, 2015. Television.

Oliver, Mary Beth and Arthur A. Raney. "Entertainment as Pleasurable and Meaningful: Identifying Hedonic and Eudaimonic Motivations for Entertainment Consumption." *Journal of Communication,* vol. 61 no. 5, Oct. 2011, pp. 984-1004.

Orange Is the New Black. Netflix, 2013. Film.

Ott, Brian L. "'I'm Bart Simpson, Who the Hell Are You?' A Study in Postmodern Identity (Re)Construction." *The Journal of Popular Culture* 37.1 (2003): 56-82. Web

Pecchioni, Loretta L., Kevin B. Wright, and Jon F. Nussbaum. "Life-Span Communication: Perspective and Methodology." *Life-Span Communication.* New York: Routledge, 2005. 3-24. Print.

Poniewozik, James. "The New *Arrested Development* Is Dark, Uneven, and Frustrating. Can We Have Another?" *TIME.* Time Inc., 29 May 2013. Web. 12 December 2016.

Powell-Hopson, Darlene, and Derek S. Hopson. "Implications of Doll Color Preferences Among Black Preschool Children and White Preschool Children. *Journal of Black Psychology,* 14(2), 57-63. 1988. doi:10.1177/00957984880142004

Rabinovitz, Lauren. "Animation, Postmodernism, and MTV," *The Velvet Light Trap,* Number 24, Fall: 99-100.

Rachlinski, Jeffrey J., Sheri Johnson, Andrew J. Wistrich, and Chris Guthrie. "Does Unconscious Racial Bias Affect Trial Judges?" *Notre Dame Law Review,* 2009. 84(3), 1195.

Ricard, Sarah. "D.C. Insiders Call *Veep* the Most Realistic Show About Politics." rottentomatoes.com N.p., 29 Mar. 2014. Web. 17 Dec. 2016.

Salvato, Nick. *Obstruction*. Duke University Press. N.p.: n.p., 2016. Print.

San Filippo, Maria. *"Transparent* Family Values: Unmasking Sitcom Myths of Gender, Sex(uality), and Money." *The Sitcom Reader: America Re-viewed, Still Skewed*, edited by Mary M. Dalton and Laura R. Linder, SUNY Press, 2016, pp. 305-318.

--. *The B Word: Bisexuality in Contemporary Film and Television*. Indiana University Press, 2013. Print.

Schwan, Anne. "Postfeminism Meets the Women in Prison Genre Privilege and Spectatorship in *Orange Is the New Black*." *Television & New Media* 17.6 (2016): 473–490. *tvn.sagepub.com*. Web.

Sepinwall, Alan. *"BoJack Horseman*: Reviewing every season 3 episode of Netflix's best show." *Uproxx*. N.p., 26 July 2016. Web. 18 Dec. 2016.

--. "How the Sad but Silly *BoJack Horseman* Became one of TV's Very Best Shows." *Uproxx*. N.p., 15 July 2015. Web. 18 Dec. 2016.

--. "Review: 'Arrested Development' On Netflix is Hilarious At Times,

--. "Reviewing Every *Unbreakable Kimmy Schmidt* Season 2 Episode." *Uproxx N.p.*, 18 April 2016. Web. 3 Nov, 2016.

Shelton, Lynn. *"Master of None." Ladies and Gentleman*. Netflix, 6 Nov. 2015. Television.

Sloterdijk, Peter. *Critique of Cynical Reason*. Minneapolis: U of Minnesota, 1987. Print.

Stanley, T.I. "Sitcoms: TV Doesn't Know Whether to Laugh or Cry." *Advertising Age*. 3 May 2004. Web.

Sullivan, J. Courtney. "Review: *Orange Is The New Black: My Year in a Women's Prison*, by Piper Kerman." *Chicago Tribune*. N.p., n.d. Web. 1 Nov. 2016.

Tartakovsky, Margarita. "Media's Damaging Depictions of Mental Illness." *Psych Central*. N.p., 17 May 2016. Web. 18 Dec. 2016.

---*The Ecstasy of Communication*, New Edition. N.p.: MIT, 1987. Print.

Tufayel, Ahmed On 1/5/17 at 11:05. "These Are the Top 25 Original Streaming Shows of 2016." *Newsweek* 5 Jan. 2017. Web. 11 Apr. 2017.

Silvan Tomkins. "Affect Theory." *Approaches to Emotion*. By Klaus R. Scherer and Paul Ekman. Hillsdale, NJ: L. Erlbaum Associates, 1984. N. pag. Print.

The Mindy Project. FOX. 25 September 2012. Television.

The Mindy Project. Hulu. 15 September 2015. Television.

Wallenstein, Andrew. "*Orange Is the New Black* Trending Stronger Than *House of Cards*." *Variety*. N.p., 5 June 2014. Web. 28 Nov. 2016.

Wallenstein, Andrew. "Long Live Zombie IP: *Arrested Development* Won't Be the Last Show that Digital Content Providers Pull Out of the Grave." *Variety* 320.3 (2013): 34. Print.

Whal, Otto F. "Stop the Presses. Journalistic Treatment of Mental Illness." In Lester D. Friedman (Ed.) *Cultural Sutures. Medicine and Media*, 2004, pp. 55-69. Durheim, NC: Duke University Press.

Winch, Alison. *Girlfriends and Postfeminist Sisterhood*. Palgrave Macmillan UK, 2013. Print.

INDEX

186, 187. *See also* gender.

Sex in the City, 174, 185

sexual assault, sexually abused,
sexual violence, 38, 81,
87, 95, 97, 98, 101, 102,
103, 104, 124, 140, 143

    rape, 97, 120

    sex crime, 119

sexual, sexuality, 2, 37, 39, 82, 83,
85, 86, 89, 90, 91, 92, 93,
123, 124, 126, 128, 129,
131, 132, 133, 140, 141,
144, 175, 176, 181, 183
184, 185, 186, 187

    bi, bisexual, bisexuality,
26, 81, 83, 84, 86, 89, 90,
91, 92

        biphobia, 92

    gay, 36, 84, 86, 89, 122,
128, 129

    heterosexual,
heterosexuality, 84, 128,
129, 173, 177, 179, 183,
205

    homosexual,
homosexuality, 86, 124,
140

homophobia, 86

    hypersexual, 75

    infidelities, 187

    lesbian, 81, 84, 85, 86,
90, 92, 109

LGBTQ, 81, 83, 84, 86, 89, 92,
93, 94

monogamy, monogamous, 180,
186

promiscuity, 183, 186

sexual liberation, 121, 122, 126,
127, 131,

queer. *See* gender

trans, transgender. *See* gender.

Shameless, 67-79

Shawkat, Alia, 6, 7. See also
Arrested Development.

Sheen, Martin, **121**, 121. See also
Grace and Frankie.

Sherman-Palladino, Amy, 18.
See also *Gilmore Girls.*

Showtime, 5, 15, 25, 68, 74, 191

Simpsons, The, 15, 132

social class, 2, 68, 82, 83, 149,
150

    lower-class, 74

    lower-middle class (adj),
70, 71, 73

    lower-working class (adj),
67

    lower tiers, 78

    middle-class (adj.),
middle class (noun), 68,
149

    upper ends (of social
class system), 67

sphere, 109, 186, 189, 192, 193,
200, 205

    private (domestic,
intimate), 154, 189, 197,
198

    public, 53, 197, 198

Star Wars, 21

stereotype(s), 43, 60, 77, 78, 108,
120, 122, 123, 125, 126,
130, 131, 133, 136, 138,
140, 142, 144, 145, 146,
147, 160, 161, 162, 164,
166, 171, 177, 180, 182,
187, 188

stigma(s, tization, tized), 96, 98,
102, 164, 165, 166, 171,
172, 183

Stiller, Ben, 11. See also *Arrested
Development.*

Made in the USA
Middletown, DE
25 April 2017